The Passing of Spanish
Traditionalism

The Passing of Spanish Traditionalism

Deprivation, Transformation, Credence

Lawrence J. Pinnie

VANTAGE PRESS
New York

FIRST EDITION

Copyright © 1996 by Lawrence J. Pinnie

Manufactured by Vantage Press, Inc.
516 West 34th Street, New York, New York 10001

Printed in the United States of America

Library of Congress Catalog Card No.: 95-90395

0 9 8 7 6 5 4 3 2 1

To myself, for the devotion and persistence
I never knew I possessed

Contents

List of Tables   xi
Preface   xiii

    Introduction: The Cultural Components   1
    Selected Cultural Factors   3
    Development of a Profile   5
    Endnotes   7
PART I: TRADITIONAL SPAIN: THE SPANISH WAY
    OF LIFE DURING THE SECOND REPUBLIC
         (1931–36)
  1. Economic Context   11
    Political Policies   11
    Foreign Contacts   13
    Living Standards   15
    Types of Occupations   18
    The Quality of Life   20
    Conclusions: Economic Patterns and Life
      Conditions Under the Republic   22
    Endnotes   24
  2. Regional Diversity   25
    Political Policies   25
    The Assimilation of Local Character   28
    Local Spirit   31
    The Status of National Unity   33
    Conclusions: Regional Diversity and the Status
      of National Unity Under the Republic 35
    Endnotes   36

3. Church Relationships   38
   Political Policies   38
   Attendance at Mass   43
   Memberships in the Religious Orders   44
   Contacts with the Clergy   45
   Religious Sentiments   47
   Conclusions: Church Relationships Under the
       Republic   49
   Endnotes   51
4. Educational Structure   53
   Political Policies   53
   Education Financing   56
   Flexibility in Program Offerings   58
   Enrollments   60
   Graduations from Institutions of Secondary and
       Higher Education   63
   Conclusions: Educational Orientation Under
       the Republic   65
   Endnotes   66
5. Summary: Spanish Life Under the Republican
       Regime   68
PART II: TOWARD NEW LIFEWAYS: THE SPANISH
WAY OF LIFE DURING THE FRANCO PERIOD
       (1960–1975)
6. Economic Context   75
   Political Policies   75
   Foreign Contacts   78
   Living Standards   80
   Types of Occupations   84
   The Quality of Life   86
   Conclusions: The Impact of Tourism During the
       Franco Period   91
   Endnotes   93
7. Regional Diversity   95
   Political Policies   95
   The Assimilation of Local Character   97

Local Spirit 101
The Status of National Unity 103
Conclusions: National Integration During the
    Franco Period 105
Endnotes 107
8. Church Relationships 108
Political Policies 108
Attendance at Mass 110
Memberships in the Religious Orders 114
Contacts with the Clergy 116
Religious Sentiments 119
Conclusions: Church Relationships During the
    Franco Period 122
Endnotes 124
9. Educational Structure 125
Political Policies 125
Education Financing 128
Flexibility in Program Offerings 132
Enrollments 135
Graduations from Institutions of Secondary and
    Higher Education 140
Conclusions: Educational Orientation During
    the Franco Period 143
Endnotes 145
10. Summary: Spanish Life Under the Franco Regime 147
PART III: COMPARATIVE ANALYSIS OF SPANISH
                LIFEWAYS
11. Economic Context: The Impact of Tourism 153
A Comparative Review of Foreign Contacts 153
A Comparative Review of Living Standards 155
A Comparative Review of Employment 156
A Comparative Review of The Quality of Life 157
12. Regional Diversity: The Effects of
      Administrative Controls 160
A Comparative Review of Local Character 160
A Comparative Review of Local Spirit 161

A Comparative Review of the National Unity 162
13. Church Relationships: The Effects of
Government Regulations 164
A Comparative Review of Attendance at Mass 164
A Comparative Review of Religious Orders 165
A Comparative Review of Clerical Contacts 166
A Comparative Review of Religious Sentiments 167
14. Educational Structure: Productivity of the
Respective Systems 169
A Comparative Review of Educational
Expenditures 169
A Comparative Review of Program Offerings 170
A Comparative Review of Enrollments 172
A Comparative Review of Graduations 173
15. Summary: The Transformation of the Spanish
Way of Life 176

Index 191

List of Tables

1. Tourist Statistics, 1931–34   14
2. Increments for Primary Education, 1931–36   57
3. Statistics on Education, 1930–35   62
4. Tourist Development, 1960–75   81
5. Percentage of Work Force, 1960–73   85
6. Percentage of Revenues Spent on Education, 1960–74   130
7. Growth in Educational Expenditure, 1960–75   131
8. Statistics on Education, 1960–70   137
9. Children at School and Number of School-Age Children, 1960–66   138
10. Students Registered in Higher Education, 1960–67   139
11. Enrollments and Graduations in Higher Education, 1960–67   141
12. Background of Students at the Bachillerato Level, Early 1970s   142
13. Comparative Analysis of Selected Cultural Factors   177–87

synthesize information on specific areas of social action in this era. From a pragmatic viewpoint, isolated cultural descriptions have little worth and meaning unless they are integrated into a comprehensive view. I am convinced that restricted reporting on Spanish society has created a cultural lacuna—a tendency to evade a realistic and inclusive description of social developments in contemporary Spain. In short, the way of life of the Spanish people has received much too little attention and discussion in existing publications, with the direct consequence that incomplete interpretations and conclusions are being accepted and acted upon by the general public and academic community alike.

The remarkably limited sociological treatment of the Franco era is not only significant for scholars in the field of social research; it also directly affects such areas as language education, intercultural communication, tourism, foreign service, international business, and the many organizations that must rely on personal contact and cross-cultural interpretations for the effective discharging of their responsibilities. In this light, the profile developed in this book is designed to help meet the practical needs of national and international sectors for a better understanding of the overall cultural tradition and character of the Spanish people. I have tried to identify and highlight essential developments in the societal patterns of Spain for the purpose of allowing the reader to gain an accurate knowledge of Spanish thought and behavior. The relevance of these profiles lies in the identification of values, traits, and traditions that directly and indirectly condition Spanish behavioral patterns.

As a teacher of Spanish as a foreign language, I have always been especially concerned with the availability of data on Spanish culture. Since World War II, the inclusion of cultural information in language programs has received endorsement from linguists and educators alike. As a result of this relatively recent concern for attention to cultural development in the language classroom, the importance of identifying the contemporary living patterns of the target society as a means of securing a full understanding of its language has had enormous impact on the contexts of curricula, materials, and pedagogical strategies in American schools. Thus, the principal beneficiaries of documentation of the way of life in contemporary Spain may well be teachers of Spanish as a foreign language at the university and secondary levels, who depend heavily upon the availability of cultural data to develop the cultural content of their lessons.

In an attempt to offset the diffused treatment of the Spanish way of life in existing publications, the current text seeks to identify, synthesize, and compare specific aspects of Spanish culture between the years 1931 and 1975 in order to provide the transitional link between "traditional" and "modern" Spain essential to an accurate portrayal of contemporary Spanish life. From the broadest perspective, it is hoped that this profile may serve to expedite international communication and cross-cultural understanding.

I have tried in this project to include the most appropriate facts on life in Spain in a period of time I am certain will be considered down through the ages as one of the most significant in the continuum of Spanish society. In the three parts of this book, I have attempted to establish for the reader an exact and inclusive description of major developments in the area of social interaction. If this report initiates discussion and appreciation of the dramatic changes in the lives of Spanish people in terms of living standards, social attitudes, educational practice, religious perception, and regional particularism, I will feel that this effort has been amply rewarded.

As a special acknowledgment, I am particularly appreciative of Dr. Eliane Condon for her candor in guiding me through the embryonic stage of this project. She not only provided excellent counsel and effective editing, but her critical insights played a major role in the evolution of the manuscript. Indebtedness of a special nature is also extended to Dr. Debbie Louis, who carefully read and edited two versions of the manuscript and gave them clarity, which was fundamental to the publication of this book.

My gratitude on the personal level is extended to many friends, colleagues, and family. Among those who have helped me with some aspect of structural preparation are John Ritter, Marcia Dunn, and Joseph Woll. I should like to thank Terri Ciliberto and Lynda Pflugfelder, who labored long hours as typing aides. My brother Anthony contributed organizational information and ideas that ultimately added perspective to my investigation. I am deeply grateful to my father for his untiring devotion and support in this, as in all of my endeavors.

The Passing of Spanish Traditionalism

Introduction: The Cultural Components

Contemporary Spain is a nation in transition. The traditional image previously associated with Spanish society is disappearing rapidly. Scholars and scientists alike have attested to the importance of the transformation that Spain has undergone in the past three decades.

Stanley G. Payne refers to this evolution as "the Spanish aspect of the common modern dilemma of transforming a largely agrarian society into a predominantly urban, industrial community."[1] The lifeways of each Spaniard, as well as the national identity of the population, have been deeply affected by this new development, as the very attitudes, values, and traditions of Spanish society have become modified in response to significant change in environmental conditions.

The contemporary face of Spain reflects trends that were initiated with the access of Generalissimo Francisco Franco to power in 1939. In fact, many of the modifications undergone by Spanish society were inaugurated during the years of the Franco regime and may be directly related to the policy actions of his administration. Indeed, the model of the Franco administration has been decisive in reshaping the behavioral patterns of the people even to the extent of altering the national character of Spain. The significance of policies implemented by the Franco regime and their impact on the social structure of Spain is emphasized by Rhea

Marsh Smith, who stated that "he is the first Spaniard to guide the destinies of Spain since the era of Ferdinand and Isabel."[2]

Under the circumstances, it is appropriate to conclude that there is a particular need for analysis of the various specific aspects of the social process during the Franco era in order to understand fully the social modifications that occurred during and as a result of that era. It should be noted, however, that a comprehensive and accurate portrayal of modern-day Spain cannot be formulated without taking into account the potential distorting effect of political influences in the weighing of cultural factors. Hence, this text undertakes the unique task of untangling the strands of domestic events from the political trends of the Franco period for the purpose of illuminating distinct cultural patterns.

In order to attain this goal, the scope of the text is restricted to an examination of those specific cultural areas that have been established historically by renowned scholars as most significant and expressive of the lifeways of the Spanish people. Stanley G. Payne, Max Gallo, Richard Herr, Benjamin Welles, George Hills, and Américo Castro are among the prominent writers concerned with the perspective of Spanish society who have particularized cultural patterns. The analytical approaches frequently employed by these authors to depict social trends are vitally relevant to clarifying current and future developments in Spanish social structure. Their social-scientific approaches emphasize identification of social change in Spain as requiring an examination of interrelated factors—the influence of political, economic, religious, and intellectual activities and events as they interact to produce specific social and cultural outcomes. Although these general categories provide a structural guide to this volume in respect to the long period of Spanish society before its abrupt change, particular features of each have been selected for more detailed analysis in respect to the contemporary era.

The primary objective of this project is to review historical political contexts and identify those specific economic, geographical, religious, and educational factors in the Franco era that appear to have resulted in a modification of the "traditional" way of life in Spain. The changes that have emerged in the Spanish way of life are also described in contrast with "traditional" patterns. The overall effort is intended to present an accurate and comprehensive description of the "Spanish character"—values, beliefs, and behavior patterns—in contemporary times.

Selected Cultural Factors

The common elements selected to guide this analysis are related to four spheres commonly considered by social scientists and writers alike as contributing to the way of life of the Spanish people: economic context, regional diversities, church relationships (with the state and with the people), and educational structure. In developing a profile of contemporary Spanish life, each of these spheres is considered and analyzed separately in the context of specific, selected cultural factors.

In terms of its potential effect on social trends, the economic development of a nation is generally considered most significant. Accordingly, a comprehensive and accurate portrayal of the life of Spanish society cannot be formulated without first taking into account the nature and scope of its economic context. The review of economic conditions focuses on (1) political policies; (2) foreign contacts; (3) living standards; (4) types of occupations; and (5) the quality of life. The nature and development of the tourist industry are also reviewed as specific features of the Spanish economy.

It has often been said that Spain, because of its regional individuality, is a land of many faces. Regional particularism as it is conceptualized in Spain is discussed here in terms of territorial sentiments and the respective problems that these entities encounter in relating to the national whole. Throughout Spanish history, three geographical regions have remained attached to local traditions and have provided the leadership in matters of regional nationalism, namely, Galicia, the Basque provinces, and Catalonia. Analyses of the unique cultural patterns and the position of each of these three territorial entities in relation to the state bring to light specific regional variations of the Spanish way of life. The discussion of regional sentiments and differences focuses on four factors: (1) political policies; (2) the assimilation of local character; (3) local spirit; and (4) the status of national unity. These inquiries disclose local characteristics and aspirations, as well as the relationship of these factors to the workings of the national government.

Spanish historians have often remarked that for centuries the Catholic religion has been a major determinant of Spanish culture. Consequently, the overwhelming importance of clericalism in Spain requires a detailed analysis. In order to determine the nature and scope of religious patterns and relationship of the church to the state and to the people, the following factors are reviewed: (1) political policies; (2) attendance at mass; (3) memberships in the religious orders; (4) contacts with the clergy; and (5) religious sentiments. The data from these analyses identify the attitudes, behaviors, and concerns of Spaniards toward the church, as well as the constitution and character of religious institutions.

4

Education in Spain, from the elementary through the university levels, has always been the responsibility of the central government. To gauge the productivity of the centralized educational system during the Franco years, both the qualitative and quantitative aspects of education must be considered. Thus, data are presented on: (1) political policies; (2) education financing; (3) flexibility in program offerings; (4) enrollments; and (5) graduations from institutions of secondary and higher education. In this way, the administrative aims, the essence of the curriculum, the schooling experience of students, and the overall orientation of Spanish schools can be determined.

The relationships of the specific cultural factors listed above to the central spheres of economic development, regionalism, church relationships, and educational structure provide a comprehensive portrayal of the outlook and lifestyle of the Spanish people.

Development of a Profile

The ultimate goal of this volume is to pursue a systematic investigation to gain knowledge of the Spanish way of life. Consequently, the presentation of unique cultural facts about everyday living patterns in Spanish society is carefully organized to highlight their interrelationships and concurrent development over time. In order to denote clearly major changes in the traditional way of life in Spain, the organizational plan provides for a chronological comparison of the specific cultural factors under analysis:

A way of conceiving history as a reflection of a way of life is only a fragment of analyzing the way Spaniards are situated with their own life. One must extract periods of time (to stand at a distance) in order to perceive its form (way of life) and functioning.[3]

The four social spheres and the respective cultural factors previously outlined are examined in the context of two political periods: first, the period just prior to the Franco regime; and second, the latter part of the Franco era, specifically the period between 1960 and 1975. Needless to say, the separate policies of the two regimes in respect to each sphere under review were shaped by their political philosophies and by the specific historical circumstances in which they rose to power. In the light of contrasting philosophies, each social analysis is preceded with a survey of major political policies affecting that area to allow the reader to note the political conditions under which social change took place.

The pre-Franco period corresponds to the era of the Second Republic (1931–36), a period of time during which Spanish society exhibited a lifestyle scholars associate with what is known as "traditional Spain." The 1960–75 period represents the last fifteen years of the Franco regime, including the years of major public policy actions to which major changes affecting the life of the people are generally attributed.

These separate analyses of the four societal spheres yield two independent profiles of the Spanish way of life—one of traditional, pre-Franco society in part 1 and one of contemporary society in part 2. In part 3, a comparison of these profiles permits the identification and description of specific changes that occurred in the traditional way of life during the Franco era, producing a conclusive profile of contemporary Spanish life and allowing for enlightened interpretation of the *meaning* of objective behavioral characteristics.

New developments evolving during the Franco era in the areas of the economy, regionalism, religion, and education, as identified in this text, have been decisive in reshaping societal patterns of the Spanish people. The emergence of precise, current data on the Spanish community, given a more accurate contextual framework than has previously been available, may now be expected to provide a source of continuing reliability in the interpretation of Spanish thought and behavior.

Endnotes

1. Stanley G. Payne, *Franco's Spain* (New York: Thomas Y. Crowell, 1967), p. 83.
2. Rhea Marsh Smith, *Spain: A Modern History* (Ann Arbor: University of Michigan Press, 1965), p. 500.
3. Américo Castro, *The Spaniards: An Introduction to Their History*, translated by Willard F. King and Selma Margaretten (London: University of California Press, 1971), p. 24.

PART I

Traditional Spain: The Spanish Way of Life During the Second Republic (1931–36)

This part of the book provides a profile of Spanish lifeways during the years of the Second Republic, a period of time scholars associate with what is known as "traditional Spain." Its contents focus on the following issues between the years 1931 and 1936: economic conditions and development, the regional situation, relationship of the church to the state and to the masses, and the educational structure. These central spheres are reviewed in respect to specific cultural factors appropriate for an accurate description of traditional living patterns of the period. Each of these spheres is preceded by a review of the policies implemented in these respective areas during the republican years for the purpose of noting the political context of specific cultural developments during this era.

9

1

Economic Context

Economic trends and standards are inseparable from understanding a community's way of life. In the case of Spain, economic development dramatically influenced the pattern of social development between the years 1931 and 1936. With political policies as a prelude, the Spanish economy during the years of the Second Republic may best be assessed through an analysis of the nature and scope of foreign contacts and capital, the standard of living, the job market, and the quality of life.

Political Policies

At the outset of the Second Republic, Spain was an isolationist nation with a rural economy. In traditional fashion, the efforts of the Republic in respect to economic development reflected an overriding concern with improvement of conditions through the nationalization of agricultural production. The Republic sought to reshape the economic structure by constitutional decrees, agricultural reform measures, and the active encouragement of traditional practices.

Title 3, chapter 2 of the Spanish Constitution of 1931 established the economic format of the Second Republic. Article 44 stated:

All wealth of the country, whomever the owner might be, is subordinated to the interests of the national economy and the support of public burdens, according to the constitution of laws.

The possession of all types of wealth is liable to obligatory expropriation to serve the mediation of adequate social reimbursement, unless directed differently by a law approved by the absolute majority vote of the Cortes.

By the same requirements property is subject to being nationalized.

Public services and exploitations that affect the common interest are subject to nationalization in cases where social necessity requires it.

The State by law shall have the right to intervene in the exploitation and coordination of industries and commercial undertakings when the nationalization of production and the interests of the national economy necessitate it.

In no case shall the government be faulted for the confiscation of property.[1]

Article 47 reinforced this theme:

The Republic shall protect the peasant and to this end shall legislate, among other matters, on the discharging of all duties on domestic inheritance, agricultural credit, reimbursement for crop failures, production and consumption cooperatives, investment accounts, agricultural schools and experimental farms, irrigation works, and rural communication routes.

The Republic shall protect fishermen in the same manner.[2]

Title 6, addressing administrative structure, stated in article 93:

A special law shall regulate the creation and the function of advisory agencies and economic ordinances of the Administration, the Government and the Cortes.[3]

Leaders of the Republic believed that in order to raise the economic level of the general population it was necessary to redistribute large landholdings. In 1932, the Agrarian Reform Law was enacted to expropriate large estates and redistribute them to the peasants in the form of smaller holdings. The law decreed that all land beyond an established limit was liable to expropriation, with compensation granted on the basis of its assessed value.

From 1931 through 1936, the Republic also sought to minimize its economic dependence on foreign countries, a policy that was felt to be essential to stabilization and expansion of internal economic resources. In essence, the government continued the autocratic course Spain had traditionally followed, making no significant enactments to encourage foreign capital investment. In accordance with the Republic's policy of regional loyalty, the administration also continued the pattern of concentrating commercial and industrial development in the northern, peripheral region.

Thus, the economic policies of the Republic demonstrated the regime's desire to improve living conditions through centralized planning and expansion of the rural economy. Specifically, the following actions underscored the economic priorities of the Republic between the years 1931 and 1936: nationalization of large estates, redistribution of land to peasants, elimination of foreign influence, maintenance of a self-sufficient economy, and concentration of industrial development in northern areas.

Foreign Contacts

Spain's economic structure at the time of the Republic was agrarian and based on a philosophy of self-sufficiency. Economic policies clearly demonstrated that governmental attention focused on the rural economy, where agricultural

Table 1
Tourist Statistics, 1931–34*

Year	Number of Tourists	Growth Rate
1931	187,000	———
1932	201,914	7.8%
1933	200,346	0.8%
1934	190,830	4.7%

* Instituto Nacional de Estadística, *Datos estadísticas de 1952* (Madrid: Dirección General del Turismo, 1953), p. 12.

reform had become a matter of survival. Republican reformers had long concurred that the resolution of agrarian discontent and distress lay in a self-supporting system of expropriation and redistribution of the large landholdings.

Accordingly, in the pre–Civil War years, among the chief items often promised by republican leaders were "the maintenance of the independence and integrity of Spain and its deliverance from invasion and economic penetration."[4] Spain, following the traditional path of isolation, had discouraged foreign contact and consequently remained closed to the capital and experience of other countries. Spain was suspicious of foreign capital, and its concern with self-sufficiency effectively restricted foreign influence in all economic matters.

In 1931, Spain received a total of 276,300 foreign visitors, but there are no figures available to determine the amount of money spent by these visitors.[5] Table 1 indicates the number of tourists with passports who entered Spain during the republican years.

Although tourism as a new and slowly developing aspect of the Spanish economy did experience a steady growth, it did not become a lucrative business. Observers have suggested that those tourists who visited Spain during this era represented a wide range of purchasing power. The majority of visitors were either upper-class Europeans who preferred elegant hotels in the resort areas or "serious-minded" teachers and students from Europe who sought inexpensive lodging. In actuality, until the 1950s tourists in Spain had been subjected to many inconveniences, for the country was not prepared to handle the "vacation" trade: road conditions were poor, the railway system antiquated, and commercial lodging offered few, if any, amenities.

Hence, Spain, following a policy of isolation and rural development, simply did not promote international contacts between the years 1931 and 1936. Consequently, foreign capital even in the form of money spent by visitors had no visible effect on economic conditions during the republican era. In fact, virtually no foreign resources existed in Spain before 1959.

Living Standards

Observers have consistently regarded the republican years to be a period of traditionalism, largely describing Spain during this period as an "underdeveloped" nation with a rural economy. The republican years have been generally characterized as a period of economic depression and low standard of living for the population. Indeed, economic activity in Spain was considerably lower than in other European countries during this period. In effect, with the burden of its traditional disabilities, Spain was stagnant.

Several reasons have been cited for the meager economic conditions of the era, ranging from the political to the psychological. Clearly, the abject poverty experienced by the middle class was a major hindrance to the development of the economy. The extreme gap between the very

15

small, very wealthy elite and the destitute masses wholly defined the economic structure at this time.

Other reasons cited for depressive conditions and the slow pace of economic progress have included the elite selfishness, political corruption, labor discontent, and the obsolescence of industrial machinery and the transportation system. However, the problem was one of values and attitudes as well as labor and income. Even among the wealthy, there was little enthusiasm for new ventures and investments. Businessmen in general were more limited in outlook and less ambitious in Spain than in other Western countries.

The wages earned by most workers at the time of the Republic did not provide them with the purchasing power needed to ensure decent living conditions for their families. The average income per citizen did not surpass $200 per year until the mid-1950s. More specifically, it was reported that the prewar proportions of families enduring "acute hardships" was above 50 percent.[6] Thus, more than half of the families in Spain did not possess sufficient clothing, food, or shelter to maintain an acceptable standard of living—in short, they did not have what were commonly referred to by sociologists as the basic necessities of life.

The period of economic depression during the republican years was for the most part due to the lack of industrial activity in the country. Spanish industrialization was a post–Civil War occurrence. Up to the close of the Civil War, the agricultural economy produced the greater part of the gross national product and represented most Spanish exports. However, because of backward technology, Spanish agricultural production was scant compared to that of other European nations. In fact, only in Catalonia and the Basque provinces, where there were beginnings of modern industrial development, did the manufacturing output (mostly in textiles and metallurgy) surpass agricultural productivity in value.

Economic depression was compounded by political instability. Assuredly, the political uncertainty of the administration affected benefits to Spanish labor written into the constitution; these had yet to be implemented in 1933, and the resulting strikes and labor unrest caused many workmen to lose their daily wages on numerous occasions. By the end of that year, labor disorders, along with barn burnings, had grown at an alarming rate.

In respect to administrative efficiency, Spain had not yet developed an organized, skilled civil service as had Britain, France, and Germany. In short, Spanish government officials did not possess the modern administrative skills to plan and manage economic programs effectively. The Republic's civil service lacked trained personnel to carry out important features of the desired agrarian reform.

The geography of the country also helps explain economic standards under the Republic. Regional fragmentation resulting from natural barriers contributed substantially to the unequal distribution of wealth among the population. While the Republic did advocate regional independence, it made no serious attempt to establish an integrated program of economic expansion for the entire nation.

Thus, with regard to the majority of the population, the republican years were characterized by poverty, low wages, and inadequate food supplies: "the original level of 1935 was judged by most impartial observers to be virtually 'subhuman,' certainly sub-Western."[7] Ultimately, the overwhelming proportions of distress among the masses affected the duration of the regime. The slowness of economic progress and the maldistribution of revenues were primary contributors to the animosity that eventually evoked civil war.

Types of Occupations

At the time of the Republic approximately one-third of the population lived in cities of over twenty thousand, while the remaining two-thirds were scattered throughout immense areas of countryside.[8] Not unexpectedly, then, agriculture accounted for a sizable share of employment during this period. In the years 1930–40, 45 to 50 percent of Spain's adult males were engaged in agriculture.[9] Overall, in 1933 the Ministry of Agriculture had jurisdiction over 4 million agricultural laborers.[10]

The traditional structure of landholding had a significant effect upon the labor market. Most landholdings were in the form of large estates owned by the influential upper class. By 1936, the population of Spain was 24.5 million. Although the majority of the people lived in rural areas, very few owned any land. In fact, fewer than half of the rural inhabitants were landowners, and many of the holdings of record consisted of small plots (hectares). A large percentage of the rural work force, therefore, consisted of tenant farmers and landless laborers. One observer noted that 4 percent of the people owned 60 percent of the land, while 65 percent of the inhabitants owned a little more than 6 percent of the land.[11]

A review of the Spanish industrial structure during the republican era indicates that the level of productivity was incredibly low and that the labor force was small and for the most part unskilled. Large-scale industry simply did not exist. It has been estimated that about 24 percent of Spain's labor force engaged in industry to earn a living in these years.[12] Labor conditions were marked by exploitation, extremely low wages, and no protections or benefits.

Social and geographical factors hampered the development of Spanish industry, as well as monopolism and selfishness on the part of the wealthy elite in commercial enterprises affecting job opportunities. Major industries consisted of textiles, metallurgy, iron, coal, shipbuilding, construction, electrical goods, paper, food processing, fertilizer, and chemical products. Textiles provided the largest source of industrial employment. Ironically, textile plants were almost totally concentrated in the northern sector of the country, namely the Basque and Catalan regions, which contained only 16 percent of the total population.

Other areas of commercial employment included fisheries, transportation, commerce, small businesses, office work, and services. In addition, national military and local police departments employed large numbers of people. In 1933, the combined total number of men engaged in police work at the local and national levels was 200,000, and the Ministry of War alone employed 139,000 men.[13]

Political and economic uncertainties brought a general increase in unemployment during the republican administration. On the whole, the unemployment rate rarely surpassed 10 percent during these years, but rural workers represented 60 percent of total unemployment.[14]

In summary, under the Republic the majority of the population derived their living from agricultural activity, although statistics on Spanish occupations vary according to the source and, in many cases, by large margins. A percentage breakdown obtained from the National Institute of Statistics shows that during the republican years 45 to 50 percent of the work force engaged in agriculture, 22 to 26 percent in industry, and 27 percent in service enterprises. In 1936, the active work force in Spain was 11 million, of which 2 million might be considered wealthy or upper middle class (doctors, lawyers, factory owners, etc.), 2 million constituted the lower middle class (shopkeepers, tradesmen, and small artisans), 4.5 million were agricultural workers, and another 2 or 3 million were employed in industrial plants, mines, or mills.[15] It is significant to note that during the republican years tourism, while a new and slowly growing feature of the Spanish economy, had not yet become a significant category of employment or national income.

The Quality of Life

Within the traditional framework of Spanish society during the Second Republic, class distinctions were very strong and explicit. In every essential institution—military, educational, commercial, occupational, and social—rigid class barriers existed. Particularly noticeable was the upper classes' lack of interest in civic problems. This rigid traditional outlook affected the entire Spanish social structure.

As previously noted, the quality of life during the republican years was consistently characterized by deplorable economic conditions throughout the country. The Spanish working class and the lower middle class were the poorest in Western Europe, with the exception of the comparable classes in Portugal and southern Italy.

Home conditions for most Spaniards were far below modern standards. Not more than one-third of the homes in rural areas had running water, only one-fifth contained a bath or shower, and fewer than 10 percent had a telephone.[16] On the whole, the proportion of homes possessing domestic appliances in all of Spain was considerably lower than that of other European nations; in fact, very few Spanish households were equipped with any kind of appliance at all:

> The houses in the villages in the interior of Spain often consist of a single room. Anyone looking in at the door can see the whole household: an iron bedstead facing the door, two or three chairs and a bench, a few primitive cooking utensils hanging on the walls, and invariably a swarm of children and dogs, to say nothing of the flies. The single door serves to light the room, to provide entry and exit for men and beasts, and to carry away the smoke.[17]

In both city and countryside, people created their own leisure activities, since the large majority of villages were isolated from roads, transportation, and water. In 1931, 270,000 vehicles (motorcycles, trucks, and cars), an average of 1 vehicle per eighty-eight inhabitants, were registered in Spain.[18] Bullfights, flamenco exhibitions, and informal gatherings were the most popular modes of entertainment. For women, marriage and a religious life were the only two roles recognized by traditional society. For everyone, daily life appears to have been an unbroken continuum of subsistence activity:

> Under the stress of poverty, the farmer presses his whole family into the task of extracting the greatest possible yield from the farm. The children cannot go to school (even if there is a school for them to go) and the women grow old before their time. The system of property and its attendant poverty preys on them all.[19]

Under these circumstances, the general conditions of life in republican Spain were reflected in such characteristics as a large rural class, rigid class barriers, poor working conditions, a high rate of illiteracy, lack of material wealth, poor transportation, and limited leisure activities. Furthermore, there were no means of improving the situation, since neither the public facilities, the private capital, nor the level of skills was available that would have made it possible to promote or carry out effective entrepreneurial efforts to develop the national economy on a scale likely to have an impact on the daily lives of the Spanish people.

Conclusions: Economic Patterns and Life Conditions Under the Republic

The republican era may be characterized as one of prevalent economic depression directly attributable to governmental policies that followed the traditional path of isolation and dependence on rural development. The regime did attempt to improve the quality of life for its people by initiating agricultural reforms and fostering self-sufficiency in the economy. Rather than producing the desired effect, however, government action during those years did in actuality inhibit both the financial and social developments of the country.

Up to the end of the Civil War, the agricultural economy constituted a larger part of the gross national product and accounted for most Spanish exports. As may logically be expected, agriculture also represented the major share of employment (between 45 and 50 percent). The 1932 Agrarian Reform Law, which nationalized landholdings previously in the hands of wealthy landowners, was intended to help the agricultural classes in Spain. While it did redistribute most acreage of land among the people, nevertheless the law failed to achieve its primary goal, as may be noted from unemployment statistics at that time:

60 percent of the unemployed consisted of rural workers. This failure may be attributed in great part to the regime's inability to implement the program of agrarian reform through lack of managerial skills even at the top level of administration. The same shortcoming affected industrial development as well, which continued to be plagued with backward technology, low levels of production, and persistent inefficiency.

Nor could there be realistic hopes of achieving substantial improvement under the impossible conditions faced by the Republic—minimal internal capital, lack of foreign resources, rigid class barriers encouraging initiative only on the parts of hereditary leaders, and a tradition of fierce independence, isolationism, and abysmal poverty.

Under the circumstances, one may view the limited status of tourism as a significant index of the ineffectual economic policies instituted by the Republic. The Tourist Bureau optimistically created in 1931 did not succeed in attracting an increasing number of foreign visitors into Spain, for the country did not possess the necessary infrastructure or skills to promote the vacation trade. Those few tourists who braved these inadequacies returned to their respective countries of origin with tales of unreliable transportation, crumbling roads, and inadequate lodgings, thereby discouraging additional visitors. Consequently, it is not surprising that at no time did tourist statistics ever rise above 200,000 yearly between 1931 and 1936. Spain continued to remain closed, stagnating in economic depression and intellectual isolation.

The quality of life of the general population failed to improve noticeably during the republican era, despite early hopes aroused by the promise of reform. In the urban centers, there was no increase in job opportunities since the regime failed to stimulate new industries; in the rural areas, land had become available to the workers but without the means of cultivating it productively. In all, living conditions for the majority of Spaniards continued as in the past to be characterized by widespread poverty, deprivation, and a lack of opportunities for upward mobility.

Endnotes

1. Ramón Tamames, *Un Proyecto de Constitución española* (Barcelona: Editorial Planeta, 1977), pp. 172–74.
2. Ibid., p. 176.
3. Ibid., p. 204.
4. Gabriel Jackson, ed., *The Spanish Civil War: Domestic Crisis or International Conspiracy?* (Boston: D. C. Heath, 1967), p. 59.
5. George Hills, *Spain* (New York: Praeger, 1970), p. 321.
6. Ibid., pp. 307–8.
7. Stanley G. Payne, *Franco's Spain* (New York: Thomas Y. Crowell, 1967), p. 83.
8. Richard Herr, *Spain* (Englewood Cliffs, NJ: Prentice Hall, 1971), p. 276.
9. Ramón Tamames, *Estructura económica de España* (Madrid: Sociedad de Estudios y Publicaciones, 1964), p. 22.
10. Federico Bravo Morata, *Historia de la República: 1931–1933* (Barcelona: Ediciones Daimon, 1977), p. 363.
11. Hugh Purcell, *The Spanish Civil War* (London: Wayland, 1973), p. 20.
12. Tamames, *Estructura económica de España*, p. 22.
13. Morata, *Historia de la República*, p. 323.
14. Stanley Payne, *The Spanish Revolution* (New York: W. W. Norton, 1970), p. 134.
15. Hugh Thomas, *The Spanish Civil War* (New York: Harper, 1961), p. 49.
16. Michael Perceval, *The Spaniards: How They Live and Work* (New York: Praeger, 1969), p. 69.
17. Purcell, *The Spanish Civil War*, p. 20.
18. Morata, *Historia de la República*, p. 65.
19. A. Ramos Oliveira, *Politics, Economics, and Men of Modern Spain, 1808–1946*, translated by Teener Hall (London: Victor Gallancz, 1946), p. 227.

2
Regional Diversity

For centuries, regional individuality nurtured by ancient traditions and physical isolation has been a salient part of Spanish culture. Indeed, local particularism has remained through modern times a basic characteristic of the Spanish way of life. Examination of regional conditions in Spain and the relationship of the regional territories to the central government during the republican years focuses on three geographical areas noted for their local identity and initiative: Catalonia, the Basque Provinces, and Galicia. In respect to political policies, regional sentiments in these locations are discussed in respect to three factors: the assimilation of local character, local spirit, and the status of national unity.

Political Policies

The Republic reorganized the administrative structure of the Spanish state by extending official recognition to the geographical areas that remained attached to local traditions throughout Spanish history. To satisfy the interests of the local regions, the government encouraged the creation of autonomous provincial governments.

The Republic's official recognition of regional individuality was articulated in the Constitution of 1931. Article 1 stated:

> The Republic constitutes an integral State, to be Compatible with the autonomy of the Municipalities and the Regions.[1]

Article 8 stated:

> The Spanish State, within the irreducible limits of its actual territory, will be made up by unified Municipalities within provinces and by regions which shall constitute a system of autonomy.[2]

Article 9 stated:

> All the Municipalities of the Republic shall be autonomous in matters to which they are obligated, and elect their officials by equal, direct and secret universal suffrage, except when there is employed a system of open council.
>
> Mayors shall always be elected directly by the people or by local officials.[3]

Article 11 stated:

> If one or several conterminous provinces, with common historical, cultural and economic characteristics agree to organize an autonomous region in order to form a political, administrative nucleus, within the Spanish State, it shall present its Statute according to the arrangements established in Article Twelve.
>
> When the Statute is approved, it shall be the basic law of the political, administrative organization of the autonomous region, and the Spanish State shall recognize and support it as an integral part of its legal edict.[4]

Article 12 stated:

> The regional statute shall be approved by the Congress, always being adjusted to the current deed, and may not contain, in any case, mandates contrary to the Constitution, nor shall the organic laws of the State in matters not transmissible to regional control obstruct the authority that the Cortes recognizes in Articles Fifteen and Sixteen.[5]

Article 13 stated:

> In no case shall there be permitted the federation of autonomous regions.[6]

Article 20 stated:

> The laws of the Republic shall be executed in the autonomous regions by their respective authorities, except where an application represents a special organization, in which case the organization must comply to that which was established in its document.
>
> The Government of the Republic shall be able to dictate Regulations for the execution of its laws, even in cases where execution pertains to the regional authorities.[7]

Article 21 stated:

> The right of the Spanish State prevails in all matters not designated in the respective Statutes as the exclusive duty of the region.[8]

Article 50 stated:

> The autonomous regions shall be able to organize education in their respective languages, in agreement with the powers that are granted in their statutes. The study of the Castilian

language is obligatory, and it shall also be used as an important instrument in all the primary and secondary Centers of instruction of the autonomous regions. The State shall be able to maintain or create in them educational instruction at all levels in the official language of the Republic.[9]

In acknowledgement of the "common cultural characteristics" of the peripheral regions, the Republic sought to return significant policy-making authority to these areas. The major policies of the Republic regarding the administration of a decentralized state were outlined in the Constitution of 1931. Constitutional provisions for decentralization included the creation of autonomous regional administrative units, localized political authority, the election of local officials, respect for local culture, and responsibility on the part of the central government for responsiveness to expressions of regional interests.

The Assimilation of Local Character

Founders of the Republic were concerned by the relationship between the national state and local identities. In recognition of these cultural traditions the Republic, through constitutional provisions, reinforced localized attitudes and interests, thereby giving tacit support of sectional movements for autonomy. Historian Salvador de Madariaga, in his explanation of the profound regional sentiments in Spain, commented:

> . . . we found that the Spanish character stood out with a vigorous individualism which puts it in a class by itself in the Western world, while within the nation, regional characters stood distinctly separate with a mutual differentiation,

a mutual assertion of individualism which drove inward, into the very soul of the nation, the vigorous individualism wherewith the nation confronted the outward world. Such is the true origin of the centrifugal movements to be observed in certain parts of Spain. And it is not by mere accident that these movements occur in Catalonia, the Basque provinces and Galicia, for it is precisely in these regions of Spain that we may observe the clearest indication of a distinctive individualized genius.[10]

Specific factors that created separate regional identities included distinct regional characters, cultural histories, and languages. Observers have given particular notice to the importance of the linguistic element in the development of local identification. There is little doubt that an underlying feature of cultural particularism was consciousness of a distinct language.

Catalonia encompasses four provinces in the northeastern sector of the peninsula: Gerona, Lérida, Barcelona, and Tarragona. The particular language spoken in this sector is Catalan. During the republican years the 2.8 million people who lived in this region made up 11 percent of the total population of Spain.

A marked feature of Catalonia in these republican years was that in a predominantly rural nation, commerce and industry constituted an essential part of the local economy. Catalonia accounted for more than 87 percent of all Spanish industrial production.[11] This dominant industrial position accounts for subsequent interest of Barcelona, with the largest urban population, in the Spanish interior.

Salvador de Madariaga gave the following description of the Catalonist perspective:

Catalonia is determined to plod on the road to progress. Leaving contemplation of Eternity to the Castilian, she is well content with time, and particularly, with the present time as manifest in the sundry objects of everyday life. The Mediterranean Spaniard is not ascetic. He feels the *joie de vivre* and lives.

A Spaniard he still is, in that his nature is synthetic rather than analytic. But he differs from the two other types in that he develops along the line of talent and intellect rather than along that of genius and spirit. Thus, Catalonia is—mentally—a land of plains at a good medium level, below which and above which fall and rise the inequalities of Castilian genius. The Catalan talent is hard-working and purposeful . . . Spanish still in that it improvises, is no longer so in that it tries to refine the material thrown up by improvisation . . . [12]

The Basque native is characterized as a free-spirited individual whose sentiment is regulated by two forces: a passionate devotion to Roman Catholicism and a pseudo-historical tradition. The local language is Vascuence. At the time of the Second Republic, the Basque region encompassed the four provinces of Guipúzcoa, Álava, Vizcaya, and Navarra, situated in the northern sector of Spain. During these years these provinces made up about 5 percent of the total population of Spain, with 1.3 million inhabitants. The separate character of the Basques was conditioned by an industrial environment, profound religious sentiments, and a strong sense of individualism reinforced by a unique language unrelated to any other in the world.

Like Catalonia, the Basque area was one of few industrialized zones in Spain during the 1931–36 period. In effect, the northern, industrial sectors of the country had evolved in territorial and social isolation and did not extend their activities—or their economic impact—beyond their boundaries. Hence, although urban growth was imminent in the

Basque area, much of life in this region remained rustically segregated and self-centered.

Galicia, located in the extreme northwest of the Iberian Peninsula, encompasses the provinces of Coruña, Lugo, Orense, and Pontevedra. Its local language, akin to Portuguese, is Gallego. Between 1931 and 1936, this region was a low-income, agricultural area subdivided into small farms. Galicians made up approximately 10 percent of Spain's population during these years.

Particularly noteworthy is that Gallegos are unlike Catalans and Basques in that they do not exhibit a fierce local spirit. In this respect, some observers maintain that Galicia has never fully developed a distinctive identity of its own in that its local characteristics reveal inherent likeness to Portuguese culture. Hence, although self-sufficient and isolated, Galicia appears to have not yet developed distinctive traditions.

Through its constitutional provisions, the Republic encouraged regional particularism in the provinces, thereby promoting the growth of strong local sentiment during those years. Under these conditions, the possession of a separate language, as well as cultural traits and traditions distinct from those of the national "mainstream," resulted in equally distinct attitudes and beliefs. Taken in toto, these characteristics constituted the basis for regionalism.

Local Spirit

In the years just prior to the Republic, particularistic tendencies among the people of various regions became more pronounced. Undeniably, the vigorous regional spirit of the times stimulated a separatist orientation within each individual. The Constitution of 1931 promised to satisfy these desires and made provisions for regional initiative and interests.

In Catalonia, the Basque Provinces, and Galicia overt actions for autonomy marked the republican years. The particularist feelings of the times can be viewed as an expression of the complexity of the Spanish character: "The more separatist a Catalan or a Basque is the more Spanish he reveals himself to be."[13] Stanley G. Payne summarized the background of this regional spirit in the following words:

> By the early twentieth century, domestic antagonisms were sharpened by the emergence of political and social movements based on regional and class exclusiveness. "Regional" or "local" nationalism as it developed in Catalonia and the Basque country expressed the pride and ambition of the only areas within Spain that were beginning to develop a modern industrial society. The Catalans had a distinct historical and cultural identity of their own: after the disaster of 1898 revealed the depths of Spain's inefficiency, they began to press for regional autonomy to continue their own development unhampered by "backward Spaniards" among whom many Catalans were increasingly reluctant to be numbered. A rather similar process was taking place among the Basques.[14]

Catalonia, which had become conspicuously conscious of its cultural identity and had recently developed an overwhelming desire for separatism, vaingloriously proclaimed its locale the Republic of Catalonia. In effect, the declaration signified virtual independence for Catalonia.

Other strong feelings for autonomy were similarly expressed in the Basque Provinces and in Galicia. The Basques, a vigorous and proud people, found ample reason to neglect the central authorities. Language and religion constituted the primary influences on the Basque attitude. Their position was based largely on a revival of Vascuence and protest against anticlerical decrees (provided in the constitution) and actions.

Local spirit became evident even in areas that had not displayed previous traditions of home rule. The opportunity, simply, inspired local administrations. Essentially, differences of spirit and of character instigated regional tendencies throughout the nation. The taste for independence among the people eventually resulted in home rule movements in all three regionalist centers—Catalonia, the Basque Provinces, and Galicia.

The Status of National Unity

The Republic's attempt to satisfy regional sentiments made it especially difficult for Spain to become a unified, centralized state in these years. At the outset, the philosophy of the Republic was to follow a course of decentralization in internal administration. In respect to public policy, it made legal provisions for autonomy among sectors with "common historical, cultural and economic characteristics." Article 10 of the Constitution of 1931 permitted regional self-government in several matters of administration, while the central government retained control over matters of foreign policy, public projects, communication, and the regulation of sects. In effect, the Republic encouraged leaders of local movements to initiate movements for autonomy.

Catalonia was the first region to draw up such a statute. The term *generalitat*, a Catalan word meaning "commonwealth," was used to signify the political unity of the region. However, before accepting the statute in 1932, the central government modified it to some degree in such areas as the local control of education and language usage. Nevertheless, Catalonia gained its own executive powers, including authorization over local financing.

Given the momentum of the Catalan movement, the Basques drew up plans for a statute of home rule. However, because of administrative delays (mostly within the Basque Provinces) the statute was never officially ratified by the central government during the regime, although the record shows that the Basque region had received official sanction for this move during the course of the Civil War. As was the case with the Basque document, the Gallegan Statute for Home Rule did not reach the Cortes in time for prompt action and official sanction. The draft had received local acceptance by December of 1932, but before it reached the next official stage, the central government fell; thus, for Galicia as for the Basque region, the hope of immediate ratification was lost.

The three home rule movements in Spain illustrate the status of national unity under the Republic. By giving in to Catalan and Basque demands, the government abandoned the centralizing tradition in administration. In essence, the autonomist movements that evolved during the Republic impeded the emergence of a unified political and social structure.

The official record was variegated: Catalans, after serious consideration of complete separatism, were induced to settle for autonomy; neither the Basques nor the Gallegans received sanction for their statutes from the central government while it maintained control of the country, despite their serious concern with independence. While these provinces had gained the promise of home rule, the impotence of the central administration prohibited the substance. At the same time, local campaigns for autonomy prevented the consolidation of a state unified in either spirit or political form.

Conclusions: Regional Diversity and the Status of National Unity Under the Republic

Throughout the centuries Spain has been a land of "many faces" characterized by a particularistic orientation based on the predominance of regional affiliations. Traditionally, each man saw himself as a citizen of his region first and a Spaniard next. This local identity, reinforced if not fostered initially by the geographical, cultural, and economic diversity of the country, had successfully prevented the emergence of a collective character in the nation and of a single coherent political unit to lead the people. Consequently, it was the conviction of the republican leaders at the advent of the regime that the political and social structure of the country could only be stabilized through the perpetuation of these particularistic tendencies.

In recognition of the peripheral sectors that remained attached to their separate cultural traditions, the republican founders chose a path of decentralization in internal administration. Through its constitutional provisions, the government went as far as to support local movements for autonomy, thereby denying the need for national unity and actively promoting the further growth of local interests and attitudes. Under these circumstances, the regional tendencies already exhibited by the people of traditional territories became more pronounced, resulting in an intensification of local identities that stressed such factors as a separate language, a forceful local spirit, distinct cultural traits, and pride in one's own special heritage.

Notably, the regional centers of Catalonia, the Basque Provinces, and Galicia expressed strong feelings for independence during the republican years. Indeed, the spirited regional feelings of the times induced organized home rule movements in all three regional centers, each of which was supported by claims of cultural uniqueness. Both Catalans and Basques, for instance, considered themselves more religious, more economically productive, and more active in social matters than other Spaniards. On the other hand, a belief in their acquired self-sufficiency and traditional ways of life underlined the Galicians' pursuit of independence.

Quite clearly, the separatist movements that persisted in Spain under the Republic affected adversely the status of national unity. In essence, the regime's determination to follow a path of administrative decentralization not only prevented the alignment of local interests with the national government, but also succeeded in paralyzing republican efforts to improve living conditions in the country.

In short, contrary to the beliefs of the republican founders, the promotion of local particularism did not appear to induce a stabilizing effect on the nation as a whole. In effect, the Republic's recognition of regional sentiments made it nearly impossible for Spain to become a unified nation in the years between 1931 and 1936. The strength of local spirit and actions, particularly those in the sectors of Catalonia, the Basque Provinces, and Galicia, created insurmountable obstacles to the emergence of both a single political unit and a coherent social structure, thereby reinforcing the traditional status quo.

Endnotes

1. Ramón Tamames, *Un Proyecto de Constitución española* (Barcelona: Editorial Planeta, 1977), p. 142.

2. Ibid., p. 144.
3. Ibid.
4. Ibid., pp. 144–46.
5. Ibid., p. 146.
6. Ibid.
7. Ibid., pp. 152–54.
8. Ibid., p. 154.
9. Ibid., p. 178.
10. Salvador de Madariaga, *Spain: A Modern History* (New York: Praeger, 1958), p. 178.
11. Hugh Purcell, *The Spanish Civil War* (London: Wayland, 1973), p. 23.
12. Madariaga, *Spain*, p. 183.
13. Ibid., p. 238.
14. Stanley G. Payne, *Franco's Spain* (New York: Thomas Y. Crowell, 1967), pp. xii–xiii.

3

Church Relationships

For hundreds of years, the ramifications of divergent religious feelings and the prestigious position of the Roman Catholic church had considerable impact on Spanish life. The new Republic's approach to the religious situation was an issue that stirred the passions of all Spaniards. The data in this chapter depict the interaction between the Catholic church and the people, and between the church and the state, during the years 1931–36. In view of stringent religious policies, church relationships in that era are examined on the basis of four factors: attendance at mass, memberships in the religious orders, contacts with the clergy, and religious sentiments.

Political Policies

Religious issues were one of the primary concerns of the Constitutional Cortes of 1931. The policy intent of the founders of the Republic with respect to religion was to provide for religious liberty and uproot Roman Catholicism in general. The anticlerical campaign of the regime was aimed at reducing the power and prestige of the Catholic church, which was deemed by republican reformers as a threat to political stability. The secular position adopted by the Republic resulted in the enactment of major new legislation in the new constitution and in several separate statutes.

The Cortes clearly defined separation of church and state as a major objective in the new constitution, beginning with the dramatic statement in article 3: "The Spanish State has no official religion."[1] Explicating the meaning of this major break from tradition, article 25 stated:

No legal bases for special privileges are to be accorded to citizens because of: property, relationship, sex, social class, wealth, political ideas or religious creed—the State does not recognize henceforth titles of nobility.[2]

Article 26 stated:

The State, regions, provinces, or municipalities are not to maintain, show favor, or provide financial aid to Churches, religious Associations and Institutions.

A special law shall regulate the total extinction of the payment of the clergy within a period of two years.

Those religious Orders which, besides the three canonical vows, require a vow of obedience to an authority other than the legitimate authority of the State are dissolved. Their property is to be nationalized and used for charitable and educational purposes.

All other religious Orders shall come under the scope of a special law administered by the Constitutional Cortes and subjected to the following measures:

1a. Those religious Orders that constitute a danger to the safety of the State because of their activities shall be disintegrated.
2a. Those religious Orders that do exist are obligated to register with the Ministry of Justice.

3a. These Orders are not permitted to add or hold more property, directly or indirectly, than they need for their subsistence.

4a. All Orders are prohibited from participating in industry, commerce or education.

5a. All Orders are subjected to all the tributary laws of the country.

6a. All Orders are obligated to render their annual financial accounts to the State.

The property of the religious Orders shall be nationalized.[3]

Article 27 stated:

The freedom of conscience and the right to profess and practice freely any religion is guaranteed on Spanish soil, provided it does not transgress public morals.

Cemeteries are to be exclusively subjected to civil jurisdiction. Redistricting for religious motives is prohibited.

All denominations may worship in private. Public manifestations, in each case, must be authorized by the Government.

No one shall be compelled to declare officially his religious beliefs.[4]

In addition to constitutional legislation, other policies on religious matters were formulated in the early stages of the Republic. In 1932, the government began to reinforce the antireligious clauses of the constitution with additional laws and decrees.

On January 24, 1932, *La Gaceta* published a decree that dissolved the Society of Jesuits and confiscated its property. Article 1 stated:

The Society of Jesuits is dissolved on Spanish soil. The State does not lawfully recognize this religious institution or its possessions, residences, schools or any other organizations directly or indirectly related to the Society.[5]

Article Two stated:

Hereafter, the members of the Jesuits may not reside together, or meet or gather for the purpose of continuing their religious activities.[6]

On February 6, the government enacted a law that secularized all municipal cemeteries and prohibited religious ceremonies at burials unless specifically indicated by the deceased in a will. Article 4 declared:

Religious activities at layouts and burials for the deceased who reached twenty years of age are prohibited.[7]

On February 17, *La Gaceta* published a mandate from the Ministry of Justice requiring that matrimony be celebrated with a civil ceremony. The order further stated that "those who seek to celebrate civil matrimony are not required to declare their religious beliefs or the religion which they profess."[8] The order also mentioned that certificates and procedures for matrimony would be free.

In March of 1932, the minister of justice decreed that the Spanish people were now permitted to divorce. Previous statutes on divorce in Spain had rigidly enforced the church's belief in the indissolubility of marriage. The new law recognized thirteen causes for divorce and issued sixty-eight articles setting forth specifications and provisions for that purpose. Major grounds for divorce recognized in the new law included adultery, bigamy, husband's attempt to prostitute his wife or daughters, desertion, threat to impose grave injury on family members, nonsupport, contraction of venereal disease outside of the legal marriage partner, imprisonment of mate for more than ten years, separation by mutual consent for more than three years, and mental derangement.[9]

To enforce the constitutional statute on religious equality (article 27) and to meet the demands of the anticlericals, the Cortes enacted the Law of Religious Confessions and Congregations in May of 1933. While this statute attempted to establish equality, its major intent was to restrict the freedom of religious orders:

> The State does not have an official religion. All orders are permitted to worship freely within the confines of their churches. To worship outside of these premises shall require private authorization from the government. In no case shall there be permitted religious gatherings of a political nature in places of worship.[10]

The republicans firmly believed that by curtailing significantly the power of the church, they would eradicate the major foe of the people. Consequently, all major legislation enacted during their administration was strongly anti-Catholic in nature. In summary, the Republic's concern to set apart church and state resulted in constitutional and separate statutory provisions affirming the absence of an official state religion, freedom of all cults to worship, dissolution of the Society of Jesuits, confiscation of property of religious orders, relinquishment of state financial support for church and clergy, secularization of education, prohibition of religious burial, permission to divorce, and civil marriage.

The majority of observers of the republican years noted that the religious issue polarized public sentiment to such a degree, many have identified it as a principal cause for the

Civil War of 1936. It appeared inevitable that the Republic's actions on religious matters and the fanatical distrust of the republican government displayed by the Catholic church were two courses that must eventually collide.

Attendance at Mass

Throughout Spanish history, the people have identified with Catholicism in religious matters. However, observers seem to agree that prior to modern times the majority of individuals adhered to Catholicism only in a superficial manner and that only one-third of the population could be described as practicing their religion to a reasonable extent. Indeed, consistent attendance at mass at the time of the Republic varied greatly—as high as 80 percent in the Basque area and as low as 3 percent in the Málaga district.[11] At the same time, at all levels of society there was in the Spanish disposition a deeply rooted element of concern for religion. The bulk of the Spanish people practiced religious ceremonies—baptism, last rites, first confession, confirmation, marriage—enrolled their children in religious schools, and flocked to religious festivals.

Social scientists have noted that during the republican years the masses regarded the upper classes as the allies of the church and the attitude of the working classes toward religious *institutions* was one of resentment, viewing them as barriers to a better way of life. Nevertheless, even in his most blasphemous moments, the worker found a reverence for religion. About one of five adults attended church regularly; however, the remaining four did not necessarily hate the church. Ten percent of the population at most were considered totally atheist—the anarchists, the Masons, and the Marxists. Perhaps another 10 percent were actually anticlerical in nature. The 60 percent majority, who were not consistent churchgoers or antireligious, considered themselves Catholic and anticipated receiving a Catholic burial at death. They strongly favored baptism of their children, whom they usually sent to church schools rather than to state schools.[12]

It is generally accepted that at the time of the Republic some 20 percent of the population attended mass regularly, 20 percent were anticlerical and never attended mass, and 60 percent, while considering themselves religious, did not attend church on a regular basis.

Memberships in the Religious Orders

While the Catholic church remained a conservative institution during the republican years, the description of Spain as a "priest-ridden" country is not an appropriate one. The caricature of Spain as a land overloaded with clergy was perhaps fitting in the 1800s, when there was a ratio of about 1 priest to every 140 inhabitants. However, the number of clergy decreased substantially during the 1930s.

Although statistics on religious matters during the Republic are by no means consistent, the ecclesiastical community during that era may be described in the following manner. In 1930, with a national population of 23.5 million, there were 32,446 priests: a ratio of 1 priest to every 725 inhabitants. By 1940, in a population of close to 26 million, one found only 25,465 priests—or 1 priest per 1,016 of the population. Nearly 70 percent of these ecclesiastics came from an agricultural background, 24 percent from industry and commerce, 13.2 percent from middle-class and professional groups, and only 1.6 percent from the nobility. At the same time, there were 2,000 parishes in Spain functioning without priests.[13]

Remarkably enough, a detailed breakdown of the nature and size of the religious community reveals that the number of nuns surpassed the number of priests in these years. It was estimated that the number of nuns increased to more than 40,000, and that there were some 10,000 monks, mostly in education.[14]

Statistics confirmed in official publications revealed that the ecclesiastical community during the republican years totaled more than 80,000—35,000 priests and 45,000 monks and nuns.[15]

In summary, in a population of some 24 million Spaniards during the republican regime the clergy consisted of 32,000 to 35,000 priests of rural origin—a ratio of 1 priest for every 725 inhabitants—and a community of monks and nuns numbering between 45,000 and 50,000. Thus, while it must be kept in mind that the available statistics on religious organizations cannot by any means be considered reliable, it is significant to note that the total membership in the religious orders under republican Spain was in the vicinity of 80,000 to 85,000, or considerably less than popular opinion has led us to believe.

Contacts with the Clergy

In its traditional fashion, the primary concern of the Spanish church in the republican years was to maintain the institutional principles of prestige and power at the expense of religious and community service. Indeed, the religious vocation was considered by most aspirants primarily for personal sanctification and reverence, rather than public interest.

It is clear that in the pre–Civil War years, Spanish Catholicism was identified by the majority of the people with the propertied classes; this view was further reinforced by the obstinate attitude of the church hierarchy on political issues, which further discouraged the allegiance of the proletariat. During the republican years, the long-existing identification of the church with the elite prevented the close contact of its clergy with large segments of the masses in most communities. In the towns and in the cities, the clergy for the most part devoted their services to the bourgeoisie and neglected the concerns of the common people. In these areas the attitudes of the working class toward the clergy was one of hatred because of the clergy's alliance with the upper classes.

Undoubtedly, most clerics were more at ease in rural than urban parishes and felt alienated from the concerns and problems of the city dwellers. In the provincial towns and villages, where the meager stipends doled out to priests by the church reduced ecclesiastic living standards to the level of working people, contacts between the priests and the parishioners occurred more frequently. Hence, in rural environments, where most clerics were as poor as the townspeople, close relationships between priests and parishioners developed.

Spanish ecclesiastics in the pre–Civil War years tended to be older men with conservative views and a narrow piety that prevented them from adopting an enlightened outlook on life. Consequently, among Spanish clergymen were many who were unfamiliar with the background and daily concerns of the people in their parishes. Moreover, the administrative policy of the Republic greatly limited opportunities for the clergy to associate with the masses. At the advent of the Republic, the government declared the church secularized and took control of religious ceremonies, thereby further restricting contact between clerics and parishioners in all communities. Specifically, the Spanish Cortes made marital and funeral services civil ceremonies, and priests and nuns were not permitted to participate in social welfare work of any kind.

On the whole, the traditional perception of the clergy as a prestigious group discouraged the development of close contacts between its members and the greater part of the population. The primary concern of most clergymen was personal sanctification, not community service. In provincial areas where the living standards of the priests were similar to those of their parishioners, close relationships between the clergy and the townspeople did exist. Nevertheless, in most cases—particularly in the larger urban centers—the traditional isolationist piety of religious leaders prevented the development of any friendly association between them and the masses.

Religious Sentiments

In order to understand fully the religious sentiments of the masses during the Second Republic, one must consider the social influence of the Catholic church throughout Spanish history. For centuries all political, social, and economic issues were perceived strictly in a religious context. Sovereigns, therefore, constantly sought to control the power and prestige of the Catholic church in Spain. Under the Republic, religion had become the most heated issue in the country, with the attendant outcome that public opinion on all aspects of policy making was divided.

Republican founders were convinced that the historical power and influence of the Catholic church had hindered the improvement of living standards in Spanish society. In this respect, one of the major objectives of the Republic was to separate church and state. Consequently, anticlericalism became the official policy of the government, a stance reflected in the many specifically anticlerical items embodied in the constitution. However, many Spaniards vehemently opposed the government's secular policy. The divided sentiments of the people regarding religious matters may best be described in the following terms: the antireligious 10 percent, and with some apprehension the liberal intellectuals and the anticlericals, were jubilant at the Republic's plans, while the church-attending 20 percent and the large majority of the 60 percent non-church-attending Catholics were appalled by the attitude of the Republic toward Catholicism. Nevertheless, within the local parishes Catholics were urged not to disrupt civil order and "to respect authority."

The religious issue became the battleground of partisans of the old order and emerging liberals. Eventually, anticlericalism became so intense that it led to frontal attacks upon clergy and church property. Violence in the form of riots and burning of churches and convents erupted everywhere as a result of aroused emotions. Many of the vandals and arsonists represented the 10 percent atheistic and 10 percent anticlerical segments of the population.

It soon became evident that government legislation and the ensuing passionate attacks on church property excited Catholic sentiment throughout the country, even among its less ardent adherents. Staunch Catholics viewed these anticlerical demonstrations as persecution. The vindictiveness of the government toward religious institutions even produced a reaction among segments of the population who were sympathetic to the Republic. Even though many backers of the Republic were devout Catholics, the regime became regarded by many as not just anticlerical, but antireligious. Undoubtedly, the Catholic cause had been aided by underlying psychological factors, namely, the deep influence that the church had had in the past on the Spanish way of life. In essence, aspects of Catholic fervor and pragmatic principles significantly affected religious sentiment during these years.

Thus, the Republic's policy to isolate the church from matters of public policy polarized opinion on both religious matters and the regime, resulting in social unrest and crime—primarily vandalism and arson. In turn, legislation and the overt actions of the anticlerical segments of the population aroused and strengthened religious sentiment to the point where loyal Catholics succeeded in gaining the support of important sectors of Spanish society that constituted more than three-fourths of the total population. Ultimately, the anticlerical campaign of the Republic was a major contributor to its own eventual destruction.

Conclusions: Church Relationships Under the Republic

The influence of the Catholic church remains pervasive in every sphere of Spanish society. Historically, all public issues—whether political, social, or economic—were perceived by all Spaniards strictly in the context of religion. The intensity of this orientation was especially noticeable during the republican years, when it was exacerbated by the antireligious policies of the government.

Under the Republic, religion had become the most heated issue in the land. One of the primary objectives of the republican leaders was to achieve the separation of church and state. The republicans were convinced that it was only through a reduction of the power and influence of the Catholic church that the Spanish people would be able to achieve their potential and enjoy a decent standard of living. In this context, religious institutions and their leaders were viewed as "the enemy" and anticlericalism became the official policy of the regime. This intransigent stance was repeatedly reflected in the anticlerical statements embedded in the constitution and in the actions taken by the government against the church and its representatives. Articles 26 and 27 of the constitution explicated the prohibition of religious motives and activities in republican Spain. In 1932, additional legislation was enacted to reinforce the antireligious items of this document.

Eventually, the anticlericalism of the regime became so intense that it led to social unrest and violence among the people. It became evident that, contrary to expectations, the Republic's legislation and its ensuing frontal attacks upon the clergy and church property failed to lessen the hold of Catholicism on the land and, instead, succeeded in renewing religious fervor within the population. Hence, the very vindictiveness of the government toward religious institutions served to explain the intensity of religious fervor manifested by the Spaniards at that time. The vigorous campaign of the government to remove all Catholic influence from their sphere of action aroused strong religious emotion among the people and produced a pro-Catholic reaction even among its less committed adherents.

In effect, policies implemented by the republican regime in the area of religion were actually perceived by both devout and nonpracticing Catholics as threats to their established way of life. To this extent, then, the nation's leaders created within the religious community a unity that had not existed previously. In response to the situation, both staunch Catholics and members of the large nonchurchgoing segment of the population—totaling more than two-thirds of the people—mobilized to protect their own interests in religious matters.

The anticlerical actions of the government had denied to Spaniards access to those cherished ceremonies, services, and functions that had previously played a major role in daily life. Hence, deprived of what had been inalienable, individual cultural traditions, Spaniards rebelled instinctively against these pressures and chose, instead, to rally around their religious leaders. Thus, despite governmental intervention, religious feeling attained a greater level of intensity during that time, and Catholicism continued to influence the lives of most Spaniards, however reluctant they may have been to practice their religion.

Endnotes

1. Ramón Tamames, *Un Proyecto de Constitución española* (Barcelona: Editorial Planeta, 1977), p. 142.
2. Ibid., p. 160.
3. Ibid., pp. 160–62.
4. Ibid., p. 162.
5. Federico Bravo Morata, *Historia de la República: 1931–1933* (Barcelona: Ediciones Daimon, 1977), p. 263.
6. Ibid.
7. Ibid., p. 264.
8. Ibid.
9. Ibid., pp. 268–69.
10. Ibid., p. 316.
11. George Hills, *Spain* (New York: Praeger, 1970), p. 136.
12. Ibid.
13. William Ebenstein, *Church and State in Franco Spain* (Princeton: Center for International Studies, Woodrow Wilson School of Public and International Affairs, Princeton University, 1960), pp. 21–26.
14. Gerald Brenan, "The Background of the Agrarian and Clerical Problems," in Gabriel Jackson, ed., *The Spanish Civil War: Domestic Crisis or International Conspiracy?* Boston, D. C. Heath, 1967), p. 13.

15. A. Ramos Oliveira, *Politics, Economics, and Men of Modern Spain, 1808–1946,* translated by Teener Hall (London: Victor Gallancz, 1946), p. 436.

4

Educational Structure

The philosophy and format of a nation's school system is generally regarded as a major influence on the way of life of a people. In Spain, education has always been the responsibility of the central administration, under the jurisdiction of the Ministry of Education. The educational structure during the republican years may be assessed in the light of conditions set forth by political policies with respect to four factors: education financing, flexibility in program offerings, enrollments, and graduation from institutions of secondary and higher education. The data presented here disclose the productiveness of the Spanish educational system in the 1931–36 period.

Political Policies

In accordance with its progressive ideals, the intent of the Republic was to reorganize—and reorient—Spanish society through educational reform. The republicans felt that the traditional approach to education—education by church schools—had hindered the development of the Spanish nation.

In 1931, the provisional government reorganized the Council of Public Instruction by decreeing that obligatory religious instruction was to be abolished. Furthermore, it repealed the decree that forbade the regional language—Catalan—being taught in primary schools.

In addition, a number of constitutional declarations shaped the educational system between the years 1931 and 1936. Article 26 stated in its opening section that

the State, regions, provinces, or municipalities are not to maintain, show favor, nor provide financial aid to Churches, religious Associations and Institutions[1]

and that

all religious Orders are prohibited to participate in industry, commerce, or education.[2]

Article 48 stated:

The service of culture is the essential prerogative of the State which the educational institutions shall disperse throughout the unified school system.

Primary education shall be free and obligatory.

Teachers and professors of official education are public servants. The freedom of professorship is recognized and guaranteed.

The Republic shall legislate, with consideration of economic needs, that the Spanish people have access to all levels of education, irregardless of aptitude or vocation.

There shall be a lay system of education; education shall make work the center of methodical activity and shall inspire ideals of human solidarity.[3]

Article 49 stated:

The expedition of academic and professional titles must correspond exclusively to the State, which shall establish examinations and necessary requirements for obtaining them even in cases where the certificates of study were issued from educational centers of autonomous regions. A law of public instruction shall determine the scholastic age for each grade, the length of the scholastic periods, the contents of pedagogical plans and the conditions under which education in private establishments will be authorized.[4]

The policies initiated by the Republic were designed to improve the quality of education throughout the nation. Toward this end, the regime increased its budgetary allotments for schools considerably between the years 1931 and 1933. For example, it was reported that the financial increment set aside for primary education was 57 million pesetas in 1932 and 43.5 million in 1933.[5] The Republic also established a policy of compulsory education at the primary level. In 1931 and 1932, under the ministers of education Marcelino Domingo and Fernando de los Ríos, plans were formulated to substitute lay schools for those previously run by religious orders and to provide additional facilities to educate all Spanish children at the primary level.

The 1932 decree to disband the Society of the Jesuits effectively reinforced the establishment of the secular system of education proposed in articles 26 and 28 of the constitution. Article 1 of the decree stated: "The State does not lawfully recognize this religious institution nor its possessions, residences, schools . . . "[6] Consistent with this course of action, the Republic enacted the Law of Religious Confessions and Congregations in 1933 to reinforce article 26, 4a, of the constitution, which prohibited members of religious orders from teaching in any schools and discouraged the teaching of religious subject matter.

Further, in accordance with the policy of creating a "contemporary" system of education, the republicans encouraged the expansion of the Institución Libre de Enseñanza, the establishment of progressive programs at the secondary and university levels, and the development of traveling programs to educate the masses.

In summary, the official policy of the Republic regarding education was to secularize the schools, thereby improving the quality of education. Consequently, legislation in this area reflected the Republic's commitment to this goal, as related statutes dissolved religious orders, prohibited religious teachings, increased public expenditures for education, provided new schools, encouraged updated programs, and rendered primary education compulsory.

Education Financing

In the traditional fashion, most primary and secondary education in Spain was in the hands of church schools just prior to the republican period. In 1931, the republican founders intended to reshape the country through educational reform and, to achieve this objective, decreed that a "lay system of education" was to be established in the country. Since Spain was a backward nation, the republicans reasoned that education by church schools hindered the development of Spanish society. The new constitution severed the traditional ties between church and state; henceforth, education was to be nurtured with complete freedom from clerical input or intervention.

Educational financing between the years 1931 and 1936 indicates that the Republic was earnest in dealing with educational matters and was eager to spend freely in this area. The government, in a determined effort to improve the quality of education, increased budgetary allotments and approved plans to provide schooling for all children at the

Table 2
Increments for Primary Education, 1931–36*

Pesetas		Pesetas	
1931	14,314,090	1934	20,371,035
1932	57,290,745	1935	9,000,000
1933	43,637,411	1936	3,496,474

*Stanley Payne, *The Spanish Revolution* (New York: W. W. Norton, 1970), p. 16.

elementary level. Statistical analyses of government expenditures attest to the Republic's enthusiasm for education. Appropriations for educational matters were highest during the early republican years. The annual amount allotted by the administration for primary schooling attained its peak in 1932 and decreased steadily thereafter, as may be noted in table 2.

In the new compulsory system of education, instruction at the primary level became the major concern of the Republic, and a major effort was made to create enough schools to meet the needs of all Spanish children. Simultaneous to the massive construction program, the government closed schools previously associated with religious orders. In February of 1932, the Republic dissolved the Order of Jesuits and confiscated their property. Through their residences and colleges, it was estimated that the Republic closed a total of 194 Jesuit institutions.[7]

In 1931, the first minister of education, Marcelino Domingo, initiated plans to provide for the education of all children. According to figures on Spanish education, some 10,000 schools were erected in various locations during the first two years of the regime in an attempt to achieve this goal. Under the previous monarchy, the average had been at most 500 per year.[8] However, published figures on republican building achievements are misleading in that many edifices were considered new only to mean that they were old parish-run schools reopened as "lay schools."

While the government strongly supported elementary schooling, it accomplished very little for education at higher levels. In fact, the government did practically nothing in the way of construction for secondary and higher education. According to Franco, in 1936 there was a total of only 111 secondary schools in Spain.[9]

Clearly, the Republic made a determined effort to improve education. The premise of its founders had been to establish a democratic government through a "lay system of mass education," which required considerable expenditure. In this respect, available statistics verify the fact that budgetary allotments for education at the time were clearly higher than those expended by the monarchy. Unfortunately, the rate of spending had to slow down as other problems claimed governmental attention, and in the end, construction activity did not extend beyond two years. Nevertheless, the Republic's achievements in education were noteworthy. Encouragement of the widespread desire of the masses to acquire education was perhaps the regime's greatest accomplishment.

Flexibility in Program Offerings

The Spanish tradition in education has been described as centrally administered, programmatically narrow, and oriented to the middle and upper classes, with low standards of academic achievement, and with most professorships held by men of conservative opinions. Throughout Spanish history, religious orders played a significant role in educating youth. By the very nature of its traditions, church influence inhibited pedagogical innovations.

The social orientation of the republican regime and the specific determination of government officials to improve mass education resulted in a deviation from these long-established norms, particularly in the creation of more flexibility in program offerings than Spain had experienced under most, if not all, of its previous regimes. The overriding republican concern to provide an education for all Spanish children was enforced through legislation, and it became obligatory for children to receive at least a primary education. Education at the primary level was to be free as well. The enthusiasm displayed by government in the education of children proved to be inspirational to the masses as a whole. Directly and indirectly, people were confronted with dramatically expanded educational opportunities.

An important modification brought into the educational system by the republican government was a relaxation of the rigid centralized control of schools that had previously existed in Spain and the encouragement of local administration of public instruction. Along with increased autonomy, communities were assigned greater responsibility in the area of education, including the legal requirement to contribute to the construction of new schools in their areas. To inaugurate local jurisdiction of schools, the government established provincial councils to organize primary instruction. Still, the most noteworthy departure from traditional education was the removal from the school system of religion and instructors from religious orders. Moreover, in direct contrast to past procedures, the Spanish church was denied the privilege of being able to prevent the appointment of instructors of heterodox views to state schools.

Another innovation initiated by government officials in 1933 consisted of asking youths to assist in educating the masses "as rapidly as possible." In essence, this program of "pedagogical missions" was representative of the spirit created during early republican years. Under this plan, organized groups of secondary and university students and intellectuals traveled to remote towns and villages with books, works of art, music, and movies to give presentations and lectures on culture and civilization. These traveling schools provided the rural inhabitants with new educational opportunities and cultural exposure.

In 1876, Francisco Giner de los Ríos founded the Institución Libre de Enseñanza, which was to be the most respected secondary school in Spain until the end of the Republic in 1936. At the university level the official body associated with the *institución* was La Junta para Ampliación de Estudios. The schools that represented the *institución* avoided traditional subjects and emphasized instead the consideration of a learner's abilities in teaching activities. Progressive education was encouraged in these pedagogical centers because it served, in turn, to nurture the spirit of the Republic.

In addition to these major reforms, other significant developments include the creation of schools for Arabic studies and the inauguration of summer sessions in at least one university (Santander).

The educational system under the Republic, then, deviated from traditional systems in several respects, notably in its departure from the rigid, centralized structure of previous regimes and in the establishment of broad curricula and flexible programs designed to provide a relevant education to the entire population.

Enrollments

With the implementation of articles 26 and 48 of the constitution, the Republic was committed to the task of secularizing the school system and providing an adequate education for all children in Spain. The obligation to educate all children was a burdensome task in that replacing the schools run by religious orders in a short period of time involved both material and political obstacles. Despite its sincere efforts, the Republic was unable to fulfill its assumed obligation, and throughout the course of the regime, at no time was there a sufficient number of schools to meet the overwhelming needs of the population.

Between 30 and 50 percent of the Spanish masses were considered illiterate in 1931; more specifically, at the start of the Republic, 12 million Spaniards were considered to be illiterate and 500,000 children were without schooling.[10] At the end of the era, it was calculated that only 25 percent of all adults in Spain still remained illiterate.[11]

A survey of the student population in schools reveals that only one-half of the Spanish children of appropriate age attended school during the republican years and that few of them continued their education beyond the primary level. Among those children of school age, 40 percent attended school in 1931, and this figure had increased to 55 percent by 1932.[12] By Franco's own admission, 60 percent of school-age children were attending school at the end of the Republic.[13]

The National Institute of Statistics has produced figures on secondary education in Spain that also reflect the efforts of the Republic. Although the Republic emphasized the development of primary education, institute statistics indicate that the number of students matriculated in secondary schools increased from 76,074 in 1930 to 124,900 by 1935.[14] At that time, there were also 29,249 students enrolled in Spanish universities.[15] Table 3 provides an overview of enrollments and educational personnel during the republican years that clearly indicates that despite its determined efforts in education, the republican government could not

Table 3
Statistics on Education, 1930–35*

Year	Number of Students Matriculated at Primary Level	Number of Students Matriculated at Secondary Level for Bachillerato	Number of Students Who Completed Study for Bachillerato	Number of Teachers at Primary Level	Number of Teachers at Secondary Level (Bachillerato)	Number of Centers for Bachillerato Study
1930	2,078,696	76,074	9,656	35,680	2,052	94
1931	2,148,978	105,649	6,164	36,680	1,722	80
1932	2,262,140	114,645	7,159	49,168	2,302	93
1933	2,397,562	130,752	—	52,954	—	111
1934	2,590,389	124,775	—	46,805	—	97
1935	2,502,322	124,900	—	47,945	—	97

*Instituto Nacional de Estadística, *Estadísticas básicas de España: 1900–1970* (Madrid: Confederación Española de Cajas de Ahorros, 1975), pp. 391, 400, 402, 403, 414.

supply enough teachers to educate all Spanish children, nor could it, in fact, build a sufficient number of schools to house them.

In summary, the educational difficulties experienced by the Republic may be attributed to its attempt to solve the religious problem and improve the school situation simultaneously. By taking a secular position, the Republic forbade the activity of religious schools and instructors—educational resources it badly needed. Overall, however, it must be recognized that the regime achieved measurable impact on the illiteracy rate in the country, since the Republic found in 1931 between 30 and 50 percent of Spaniards illiterate and by 1936 had accomplished a sizable reduction, to 23 percent.

Graduations from Institutions of Secondary and Higher Education

Since the Republic had devoted itself mainly to primary education, it could be expected that the most effective results of its efforts would appear at this level—and indeed, elementary enrollments reached 60 percent in 1936, a proportion significantly higher than that achieved by the previous regime. Beyond the primary level, however, school attendance tapered off considerably, a pattern that has been consistent throughout Spanish history.

Comprehensive statistics on grades completed and certificates awarded are not available for this era. However, figures supplied by the National Institute of Statistics reveal that in 1931 there were 105,649 students matriculated in schools awarding the *bachillerato*, of whom 6,164 received certificates; in 1932, matriculation reached 114,645, with 7,159 youngsters awarded certificates. During the 1935–36 academic year, however, a mere 4 to 5 percent of the total enrollments consisted of secondary students (124,900) and only 1 percent represented students matriculated in Spanish universities (29,249). From these figures it may be estimated that approximately 5 percent of the students who completed the elementary level continued their education at the secondary level, and of those who entered a secondary program, 23 percent went on to study at a university or a technical college.[16]

Clearly, secondary and higher education remained areas of critical need during the republican years. From a political standpoint, the regime had made no commitment to render secondary education compulsory, nor did it propose at any time to implement an extensive building program for this level. Figures from the National Institute of Statistics only show an increase in schools for the *bachillerato* from 80 in 1931 to 97 in 1935.[17] The hands-off policy adopted by the Republic with respect to secondary education extended as well to the college level: the minister of education himself, Fernando de los Ríos, acknowledged the unfortunate fact that in university education, little had been achieved by the regime.

Despite educational reforms under the Republic, then, the majority of children from working-class families did not enroll in secondary schools. Those who did and those who continued beyond the secondary level came predominantly from middle- and upper-class families. In effect, beyond primary school, children from lower-class backgrounds faced a future of unskilled labor to help the immediate family in its fight for survival.

The educational reforms of the Republic primarily affected the primary level, with little development in secondary and higher education. Accordingly, a relatively small number of students attained the secondary and college levels in these years, and fewer still succeeded in obtaining a *bachillerato* or university degree.

Conclusions: Educational Orientation Under the Republic

The Spanish tradition in education may best be described as programatically narrow and oriented to the middle and upper classes. The educational philosophy of the republican regime and its implementation by government officials reflected an explicit desire to modify these long-established elitist traditional norms. From the beginning, the overriding intention of republican leaders was to reorganize Spanish society through the expansion of educational opportunities. Toward this goal, the new compulsory system of education established by the regime was designed to educate all Spanish children at least at the primary level.

Despite its constructive efforts, at no time during its tenure was the Republic able to provide a sufficient number of schools to meet the overwhelming needs of the population. The difficulties experienced by the regime in achieving its educational goals can be attributed primarily to social and economic obstacles. A large majority of the population lived in the rural areas, which tended to restrict the availability of education to the masses. In effect, the government's assumed obligation to educate all Spanish children was an idealistic but impossible task, since Spain lacked the necessary economic resources to reach—much less mobilize—the population effectively. An examination of student enrollments in schools during those years showed that only one-half of the Spanish children of school age received instruction and that beyond the elementary level this attendance suffered drastic reduction.

Aside from its sponsorship of compulsory elementary education, the republican regime generally failed in its attempt to eliminate the class-based inequalities that had plagued the Spanish educational system in previous years. Rigid social stratification was directly reflected by the lack of educational opportunities available to laboring-class families. In most cases working-class parents were unable to afford the costs of fees and texts that accompanied the enrollment of their sons and daughters in a secondary school. Clearly, the majority of children from lower-class environments did not and could not study beyond the elementary level and, consequently, faced a future of unskilled labor.

Thus, at the time of the Republic, education retained its traditional elitist orientation: only 1 percent of the children enrolled in secondary schools were of working-class backgrounds. The educational structure continued to function as a sorting system for social stratification, with primary education reserved for the working class, secondary education for the middle and upper class, and higher education for the upper class. It must, however, be recognized that the regime did achieve measurable progress in this area: as a result of governmental sponsorship of mass education, the illiteracy rate of Spain underwent sizable reduction. In five short years, it dropped from an overwhelming 30 to 50 percent, in 1931, to 23 percent, in 1936.

Endnotes

1. Ramon Tamames, *Un Proyecto de Constitución española* (Barcelona: Editorial Planeta, 1977), p. 160.

2. Ibid., p. 162.
3. Ibid., p. 176.
4. Ibid., pp. 176–78.
5. Stanley G. Payne, *The Spanish Revolution* (New York: W. W. Norton, 1970), p. 161.
6. Federico Bravo Morata, *Historia de la República: 1931–1933* (Barcelona: Ediciones Daimon, 1977), p. 263.
7. George Hills, *Spain* (New York: Praeger, 1970), p. 146.
8. Ibid.
9. Ibid., p. 136.
10. A. Ramos Oliveira, *Politics, Economics, and Men of Modern Spain, 1808–1946*, translated by Teener Hall (London: Victor Gallancz, 1946), p. 62.
11. Stanley G. Payne, *Franco's Spain* (New York: Thomas Y. Crowell, 1967), p. 100.
12. Oliveira, *Modern Spain*, p. 457.
13. Hills, *Spain*, p. 377.
14. Instituto Nacional de Estadística, *Estadísticas básicas de España: 1900–1970* (Madrid: Confederación Española de Cajas de Ahorros, 1975), p. 402.
15. Instituto Nacional de Estadística, *Anuario estadístico de España: 1960* (Madrid), p. 885.
16. Ibid., pp. 885–87.
17. Instituto Nacional de Estadística, *Estadísticas básicas de España 1900–1970*, p. 414.

5

Summary: Spanish Life Under the Republican Regime

The information reported in this part of the book, which provides a profile of the Spanish way of life at the time of the Second Republic, has focused on the following societal spheres: economic context, regional diversity, church relationships, and educational structure. However, to synthesize accurately the data on Spanish life during these years, it is necessary to examine the relationships among these spheres.

The data indicate significant societal variations that reflected in their orientation the political policies and format of the republican regime. The administrative structure of the regime itself clearly reflects the interaction of economic, regional, religious, and educational factors between the years 1931 and 1936. In the description of policy modification and resulting social development under the Republic, it has been necessary to allude frequently to the relationship between the political and the religious spheres, since the underlying factors of the religious question affected public policy action at all levels of society. The republicans explicitly prescribed the separation of church and state at the advent of their regime; they firmly believed that by restricting the power and prestige of the Catholic church they would eradicate the major adversary of the masses.

Consequently, anticlericalism became the official policy of the government.

The social effects of the regime's approach to the religious question during this period are distinct. The political stance of the Republic on religion excited Catholic sentiment throughout the nation: three-fourths of the population viewed government anticlerical actions as persecution. In effect, the various segments of Spanish society mobilized to protect a common interest in the form of the Spanish Catholic tradition. The government's rigid control of religious practice further restricted contacts between the clergy and populace, since priests and nuns were forbidden to engage in any social work at that time. The data also suggest that economic circumstances within the religious community also affected clergy-populace relationships during these years. The traditional perception of the clergy as a prestigious group prevented the development of close interaction between them and large segments of the population. For the most part, the clergy devoted their efforts to the bourgeoisie and elite, neglecting the needs and concerns of the proletariat. Moreover, the intransigent attitude of many clerics discouraged the allegiance of the working class.

The most noteworthy effect of the Republic's religious policy was on education. From the start, the policy intent of the administration was to initiate development within Spanish society through educational reform. Toward this goal, the government felt that the traditional approach of church schools, which had played a major role in educating children in the past, hindered the progress of the nation; it therefore closed schools previously operated by religious orders, to provide a lay system of education.

However, it was this secular position taken by the Republic to improve school instruction that quickly paralyzed the development of education. By forbidding the operation of schools run by religious orders, the government deprived its own effort of educational resources it could not afford to lose: throughout the course of the regime the Republic was unable to supply enough teachers or schools to educate all Spanish children, as it had originally intended.

The ramifications of the Republic's policy on religion extended to the regional sphere as well. Throughout Spanish history regional individuality has been a conspicuous part of Spanish culture. In recognition of these local traditions, the Republic, through constitutional provisions, encouraged regional interests and attitudes. Strong movements for autonomy developed in Catalonia, the Basque Provinces, and Galicia in these years. Ironically, the most distinguishing feature of the Basques was religious intensity; consequently, their movement for autonomy was strengthened by the anticlerical position of the national government. In effect, regionalist and religious policies of the regime combined to encourage the development of separatist movements.

Although religious matters motivated regional particularism to a large extent, economic circumstances also encouraged regional initiative during this period. Spain's economic structure remained agrarian and characterized by poverty and economic stagnation. The Basque and Catalan regions, however, were included among the few industrial sectors in the nation, developing local pride in the distinction of possessing a modern industrial society. Economic factors similarly inspired the Galician home rule movement; the major concern of their leaders was to improve economic conditions in their own community.

The ramifications of regional identity influenced the educational sphere as well. Home rule statutes drafted by the local sectors indicated the desire to operate their own school systems independently. Local school curricula reflected—and emphasized—the separate character of the respective regions, in both language usage and program offerings.

As would be expected, economic circumstances affected the progress of education at the time of the Republic. Quite clearly, the availability of schooling to the masses was limited during the period, as the large majority of Spaniards lived in the rural areas. In effect, Spain in the years between 1931 and 1936 lacked the impetus of industrialization, which would mobilize the population to seek educational opportunities. Accordingly, figures show that enrollments at all educational levels remained extremely low at that time.

Overall, the relationships between Spanish social patterns and governmental policies during the republican years are clearly evident. Most notable was the pervasive impact of religious matters on all other social developments at this time. The ramifications of religious controversy were felt in every major institution—whether social, educational, geographical, or economic—in the entire country.

PART II
Toward New Lifeways: The Spanish Way of Life During the Franco Period (1960–75)

This part of the book explores the factors selected for review in respect to the Franco period, to develop a profile of the contemporary Spanish way of life. Preceded by an examination of respective political policies, the four major areas selected for the analysis of conditions of Spanish life: economic context, regional diversity, church relationships, and educational structure, are examined during the years from 1960 to 1975.

6

Economic Context

Quite clearly, the Franco regime's economic plans significantly affected social patterns. The development of tourism during the Franco era had a particularly dramatic impact on social development. As has been done for the republican epoch, with political policies as precursor, the assessment of economic conditions focuses on the nature and scope of foreign contacts, living standards, types of occupations, and the quality of life.

Political Policies

At the inception of his regime, Franco maintained the traditional policy of economic self-sufficiency. It was his early decision to rule Spain as an autarchy, intending to free the economy from foreign dependence. Thus, in conformity with the traditional approach to economic development, between the years 1939 and 1953 Franco advocated isolation as the means to economic self-sufficiency.

However, international opinion—specifically, that of the Western industrial nations—perceived Spain's nationalistic tendencies as obstacles to its economic development. Deeply indebted to these nations for their role in establishing and maintaining his regime, Franco was eventually persuaded to this view and through the 1960s sought to break away from the path of isolationism in order to attract foreign capital, which would permit the expansion of the Spanish economy. Economic development in the Franco period was thereafter marked by an ambitious course of constitutional enactments and other actions.

Franco's major political policies were defined in a series of documents titled the Fundamental Laws of the State, which in their entirety represented the Spanish constitution. The specific clauses of the law that defined Franco's economic policies and objectives and controls are reviewed below.

Section 11 of the Law on the Principles of the National Movement of May 17, 1958, stated:

> Commercial enterprise, the association of men and means geared to production, constitutes a community of interests and a unity of purpose . . . and economic values shall be subordinate to those of a human and social order.[1]

Section 12 stated:

> The State shall endeavor, by all the means at its disposal . . . to stimulate the economic progress of the Nation . . . to direct the most equitable employment and distribution of public credit; . . . to intensify the process of industrialization . . .[2]

Section 11 of the Labor Law (Fuero Del Trabajo) of March 1938, amended by the Organic Law of the State of January 10, 1967, stated:

> (1) National production is an economic unit in the service of the country. It is the duty of every Spaniard to protect, improve and increase it. All factors involved in production are subordinate to the supreme interests of the Nation . . .[3]

76

Section 13 stated:

> (1) Spaniards, by virtue of their participation in labour and production, constitute the Trade Union Organization . . . (4) The trade unions are the channel of professional and economic interests for the fulfillment of the ends of the national community, and are the representatives of said interests . . .[4]

Article 10 of the Constitution Law of the Cortes of July 17, 1942, amended by the Organic Law of the State of January 10, 1967, stated:

> The Cortes shall examine, in plenary session, the acts of laws dealing with the following matters: . . . (b) large-scale operations of an economic or financial nature: . . . (e) the economic intervention of the Trade Unions and whatever legislative measures may affect the Economy of the nation to an important degree: . . . (k) the structure of agrarian, mercantile and industrial organization . . .[5]

The regime's course of action to raise economic standards through massive industrialization became a persistent one. In an attempt to improve economic conditions that proved impervious to traditional efforts, Spain began seeking advice from beyond her borders by the mid-1950s. In 1958, Spain became a member of the OECD (Organization for Economic Cooperation and Development), an economic advisory organization that reported that the nation's industries were inefficient and the country needed foreign investment to expand the economy significantly.

Under the rubric of "Economic Liberalization," the regime moved to terminate Spain's policy of isolation and open her economy to major investment from other countries. Observers considered 1959 to be the year in which the era of rapid economic growth in Spain began. Economic barriers were lifted and plans were inaugurated to establish liberal economic programs. During the 1960s the regime encouraged the massive use of foreign capital and vigorously promoted tourism. Further, the government initiated a program to channel foreign capital into what it considered to be priority areas, such as construction, transportation, tourism, steel, auto plants, and electronics.

In 1962, the government announced a series of four-year programs to provide a framework for economic expansion. These plans were designed in the context of expectations for the growth of tourism to balance the economy as other aspects of development were implemented. The First Development Plan (1964–67) emphasized overall economic growth, financed domestic programs, and specified tourism as a form of major industry. The Second Development Plan (1968–71) was designed to correct the shortcomings of the first plan, facilitating economic growth and "catering to" tourists. The Third Development Plan (1973–76) concentrated on stabilizing the economy, stressing "quality instead of quantity" in tourism, and correcting the new and escalating problems that had begun to arise as a result of the tourist trade.

Thus, the economic policies of the Franco era were formulated in response to a need to improve living conditions. Franco ultimately turned to liberal programs in an effort to attract foreign capital to accelerate economic growth.

Foreign Contacts

Economic policies implemented by the Franco regime indicated that, out of necessity, the dictator had been compelled to reverse his economic plans in the 1950s. Western politicians and economists alike began to comment publicly that the nationalistic economy was restraining development. When Western nations advised Franco that an expansion of his country's economy would require a breaking away from the traditional goal of self-sufficiency, he turned to tourism to stimulate economic development. Thus, the need for economic advances at all levels of society made possible a relatively stable transition from economic isolation to foreign-capital dependency.

The regime began to prepare an emphasis on tourism in the late 1950s. By this time, leaders of the administration were aware that politics per se were no longer the major concern of the Spanish people. Franco himself realized that the current generation of Spaniards was much more concerned with higher living standards than ideologies.

Several efforts were undertaken by the government to guide and encourage an expanded tourist trade. Improvement of highways, trains, and airports, increase in the number of hotels and lodging places, improvement in the quality of hotel services, control of types and prices of hotels, lodging places, and restaurants, and channeling of foreign capital to the tourist industry succeeded in facilitating this development. By the 1960s the Spanish tourist industry had become one of the biggest and best in the world. Indeed, the government had taken great care to develop organized, attractive, reasonably priced tourist facilities of every kind. Its achievement in hotel construction was most evident. The number of hotels, hostels, and pensions probably tripled during the decade.

Despite its commitment to traditional religious dogma, the government did not allow those considerations to interfere with the growth of tourism. In fact, hotels and lodging places were authorized by Tourism Minister Mañuel Fraga Iribarne to make available to tourists Protestant chapels and services.

More important, the attitude of the Spanish people regarding the influx of foreigners seemed to be one of acceptance. Friendliness and courtesy in restaurants, hotels, and shops were apparent both in the small towns and in the cities.

The growth of this industry under Franco is best reflected by related statistics. In the 1968 budget (which tripled the 1961 budget) close to 3 billion pesetas were allocated for the development of tourism.[6] Figures provided by the National Institute of Statistics document the development of tourism from 1960 to 1975. Table 4 depicts the increase in the number of tourists and tourist offices and money spent by tourists in four years during the Franco era. As these statistics indicate, the total number of visitors to Spain increased 500 percent between 1960 and 1975.

The tourist industry played an important role in Spain's international affairs as well. The minister of information and tourism stated that in 1964 the tourist trade had paid for "two-thirds of the deficit anticipated in our commerce."[7] More specifically, a Spanish government publication, *Spain 77*, reported that "tourism earnings covered 79 percent of the trade gap between 1962 and 1973."[8]

The Franco regime, by promoting international contacts, attracted a steady flow of foreign currency. This was, in turn, primarily responsible for the transformation of Spain's traditional economy into a progressive structure. Indeed, tourism became a major industry under Franco, and its fiscal productivity proved beneficial to Spaniards in all areas of the economy.

Living Standards

Both narrative and statistical data on the Franco era indicate that the regime's progressive policies initiated in

Table 4
Tourist Development, 1960–75*

Year	Tourists with Passports	Total Visitors	Money Spent by Tourists (Thousands of Millions of Pesetas)	Tourist Information Offices in Spain	Tourist Information Offices in Foreign Countries
1960	4,332,363	6,113,255	21,060	1,115,805	851,964
1965	11,079,556	14,251,428	45,610	2,472,092	926,991
1970	21,267,380	24,105,312	97,410	3,420,812	1,336,735
1975	27,359,337	30,122,478	158,930†	5,353,834	1,454,712

*Instituto Nacional de Estadística, *Anuario de estadísticas de turismo: Año 1976, tomo I demanda* (Madrid: Secretaria de Estado de Turismo, 1977), pp. 493, 494, 497; *Documentación básica del IV Plan Nacional de desarrollo* (Madrid: Subsecretaria de Planificación, 1976), p. 24.
†1973 figures.

the 1950s enhanced socioeconomic development and that the years between 1960 and 1975 constituted a period of substantial economic development. Economic expansion was facilitated by the administration's attempts to proceed in accordance with a carefully planned development program patterned after the French system. The efforts of the government in this area were a great improvement over the impotent, autocratic procedures of earlier years.

On the whole, economic growth occurred in direct proportion to the development of tourism as a major industry. Suspicion of the foreigner under the Republic had given way to encouraging tourist spending. In the 1960s Spain's main industry brought $500 million yearly to a nation that only a few years earlier was on the brink of bankruptcy.[9] As a result of this dramatic financial change, living standards rose considerably at all levels of society during these years. Spain's economic growth rate was impressive, despite continuing problems of inflation in the later years of the Franco era.

From a statistical standpoint, leading economic indicators in these years showed growth in most major areas. In a five-year period in the 1960s, the gross national product had risen from $9.5 billion to $13.8 billion.[10] Average *per capita* income increased from $317 in 1960, to $850 in 1967, to $1,250 in 1973.[11] Wages in Spain had increased on the average by 15 percent a year.[12] The minimum daily wage increased from 60 pesetas (about $1.00) in 1963 to 186 pesetas ($3.30) in 1973.[13]

However, the economic progress made by Spain could not measure up to the level of advances reached by its neighbors. Among Spain's weaknesses was the productivity of Spanish labor, which was extremely low in comparison to the European level and that of Western nations.

Another difficulty created by the emphasis on industrial and tourist activities in Spain was to be found in the corresponding decrease of efforts in the area of agriculture. In the official record, agricultural neglect registered significant points of weakness in the progressive economy initiated in the 1960s. Although food production increased rapidly and consistently in these years, the price ceilings curtailed profits and restricted living standards for the large majority of the farm-related populace. A farmer-owner and his family drew an average income of only $300 per year. Moreover, two-thirds of Spain's rural land was owned and operated by such farmers at this time.[14]

To some extent, the restricted opportunities offered by agriculture were offset by the new economic developments, but the latter also resulted in unexpected changes, particularly in demographic shifts and distribution of national income. Between 1960 and 1968 some 400,000 workers from farms took jobs created by the tourist industry in the southern Mediterranean and Balearic Islands.[15]

In summary, the years from 1960 to 1975 represented a period of substantial economic growth in Spain, which may be attributed primarily to a spectacular increase in tourism. As a consequence of this expansion, living standards were elevated considerably for the majority of the population during these years. Significant growth was apparent in major economic measures such as national income, salaries, purchasing power, and international trade. In combination, they describe overall socioeconomic progress as illustrated in a statistical study sponsored by the Bank of Bilbao on the Spanish economy from 1955 to 1975:

During the years covered by this study, the GNP in current prices increased by 1,238 percent and in constant prices by 211 percent. The accumulative annual growth rate of GNP at the ruling rate grew by 13.8 percent and in constant prices by 5.8 percent . . . The era of greatest expansion of the GNP was between 1960–73, in which an accumulative annual increase of 7.6 percent was achieved.[16]

Types of Occupations

With respect to the working population, the new economic trends initiated between the years 1960 and 1975 led to modifications in the labor market, among them a major shift from agriculture to industry and services. These alterations were the result of the regime's new and deliberate policy to encourage industrial growth and regard agricultural expansion as economically and politically unsound.

The consequences of this diminished role of agriculture in Spain's economy left vast rural areas virtually unproductive and confined a large sector of the population to only minimal benefits from the increased living standards that other sectors of Spanish society were enjoying. A Spanish government report in 1978 indicated that while the overall income rose by 44.54 percent, the income of the farm worker increased by only 24.28 percent.[17]

The effects of labor shifts and trends on social class were evident. Of greatest significance in respect to continuing progress, the middle class was becoming a growing sector of Spanish society. As a result of swift economic progress, much of the working-class population was acquiring the values and living standards of the middle class. The tourist industry, urbanization, and associated entrepreneurial opportunities allowed more people than ever before to develop comfortable lifeways.

Statistical accounts of the Spanish work force during these years vary from source to source but are consistent

Table 5
Percentage of Work Force, 1960–73*

Year	Agriculture and Fishing	Industry	Services
1960	41.0%	31.8%	26.5%
1973	23.0%	37.2%	39.8%

*Eugene K. Keefe, *Area Handbook for Spain* (Washington: Foreign Area Studies [FAS] of the American University, U.S. Government Printing Office, 1976), p. 294.

in denoting patterns and trends. In the 1960s some 2 million people had left rural environments for the cities, and the working population engaged in agriculture had dropped from 43.2 percent in 1960 to 30 percent in 1974.[18] Table 5 summarizes the job situation for the 1960–73 period in terms of three major categories. Data provided by the National Institute of Statistics indicate the following percentage breakdown of the distribution of employment in 1966:

Agriculture	33.3
Manufacturing	24.7
Services	14.3
Commerce	11.6
Construction	8.2
Transport	4.8
Mining and Quarrying	1.3
Fisheries	.09
Electricity, gas, and water	0.9[19]

Many Spaniards had resorted to dual occupations in order to keep pace with the rapidly changing economic structure—and inflation. Apparent prosperity among the working population was mainly due to moonlighting, overtime compensation, and family sacrifices. It was estimated in 1966 that 4.5 million workers, more than one-third of the entire work force, had more than one job.[20]

It was often reported in the international press at that time that Franco did not give serious attention to unemployment during this period of economic progress. The regime never considered unemployment to be a serious problem and consequently failed to apply major measures to regulate employment. Official figures produced by the Ministry of Labor in the 1960s indicated that unemployment was less than 2 percent, although estimates from other sources were slightly below 5 percent.[21] For the year 1975 the unemployment rate hovered between 4 and 5 percent.[22]

Overall, the labor force under Franco experienced a significant change in major employers from agriculture to industry and services. This trend was reflected in a migration of the working population to the cities, where jobs were thought to offer a better way of life. In 1975, of an estimated work force of 13.5 million, about 23 percent were engaged in agriculture, 37 percent in industrial jobs, and 40 percent in services.[23] Apparently, agriculture declined in proportion to developments in other major segments of the economy and, accordingly, in the status of the labor force. A review of the labor policies of the era indicates that this development resulted directly from deliberate government policies designed to expand the economy by emphasizing industrialization and disregarding agricultural development.

The Quality of Life

The dramatic change in the nature of the Spanish economy between the years 1960 and 1975 resulted in a significant alteration of the Spanish way of life. Indeed, economic trends during this period improved living conditions and raised living standards considerably. From a technologically backward nation devoted primarily to a traditional rural economy, Spain had evolved into a mobile, urbanized, industrial society.

The impact of structural changes on Spanish lifeways was evident in all of the major institutions—church, government, business, and education—producing growing signs of diversified values and attitudes and mobility. Spanish life became more variegated, and as progress became more rapid, its transformation became deeper; sentiments and tensions between old societal traditions and new demands were intensified. Incredibly enough, the people of Spain endured and adjusted to all of these occurrences. They devoted much of their time to adapting to the intensity of work, the task of production, and new environments, occupations, and value systems that had changed the rhythm of their lives.

Spaniards experienced a surge of material prosperity previously unknown in their country. Many people were now earning a decent wage and were eager to upgrade their material living standards. Autos, telephones, televisions, and domestic appliances such as washing machines, refrigerators, ranges, and the like—well out of the reach of the average family a decade ago—were now commonplace in nearly all working-class and middle-class homes. In addition, the apparent security and benefits characteristic of the advent of an industrial economy dramatically altered the ideals and expectations of an increasing number of the population. The views expressed by Paul Holmann in the *New York Times* on life in Spanish society in the 1960s illustrate general attitudes and the improvement of living conditions that occurred during the latter part of the Franco era:

The new generation is "conspicuously unascetic" . . . This generation is frankly impatient to share the good life of other Western Europeans . . . They want autos, affluent vacations like those enjoyed by the millions of tourists who invade Spain from spring to autumn, modern household appliances, smart clothes, and better food. If they lack the cash they buy on the installment plan.[24]

Ample statistical evidence verifies the rise in the material standard of living during this period. Figures indicate that in 1968, 53 percent of the population owned their own living quarters (assumed to be mostly apartments). It was estimated that 1 of every 25 inhabitants was the owner of an automobile, while 34 percent of Spaniards had a TV set in their home, 35 percent owned a refrigerator, and 39 percent owned a washing machine. The number of telephones per 1,000 inhabitants rose from 34 in 1955, to 80 in 1965, to 181 in 1973.[25]

The importance of the psychological implications of rapid change and economic prosperity in the era warrants emphatic consideration. Behind the demand for better living conditions was the fact that the Spanish people had long been deprived of convenience, comfort, and the trappings of success. Consequently, the most dramatic change resulting from the transition from a traditional rural economy to a progressive industrialized one was one of attitude. In a subtle but definite manner Spaniards were vastly developing liberalized values and ideals. The way they perceived their own lifeways and their traditional institutions in relation to other nations had undergone alteration as a result of increased exposure through tourist contacts, television, education, and foreign travel. Social class consciousness and mobility, migration from rural environments to the cities, and the availability of a more active social life created a cosmopolitan perspective, affecting the entire value system.

The impact of rapid demographic shifts and economic changes on Spanish society created population and capital imbalances. Industrial and business development concentrated the population and nearly all financial power within three areas—the triangle of Madrid, Barcelona, and Bilbao, a region that comprised less than 5 percent of Spain's total area but contained more than 28 percent of the population, 39 percent of the nation's total income, and 49 percent of banking and investment activity.[26]

In respect to social stratification, changes in class structure occurred in response to changes in living conditions. Class strata were not nearly as rigid as they had been a decade before. Opportunities for people to rise from modest backgrounds to influential positions in business, politics, education, and the military were increased. The key elements for class mobility were now education, affluence, and individual determination and talent rather than lineage. These shifts in the class distribution of Spanish society encouraged the expansion of the middle class. The term *middle class* was utilized to encompass a broad and growing segment of Spanish society—from families who had done well in business, government, or the professions to the large majority of modest families who devoted all of their efforts to making ends meet for the sake of appearance and respectability. Most middle-class families lived in rather humdrum, overcrowded apartments in tenementlike neighborhoods of the city. The immediate and extended family living together was still common; it usually included the head of the family and his wife and children, dependent relatives, and perhaps a lodger.

The transformations that were taking place in Spanish society during the Franco period extended to include the changing roles and status of women. Traditionally, marriage and the religious life were the only two roles considered appropriate for Spanish females. However, as economic and educational opportunities opened for women, the means to a wider range of social achievements were put firmly in place. Economic pressures and the lure of material prosperity compelled more and more women into the labor market. In ten years the proportion of women in the work force rose from 16 percent in 1955 to 25 percent in 1965.[27] In practice, however, three-fourths of working women held the most menial jobs and were paid poorly. In theory, women were afforded equal educational opportunities, but the proportion enrolled in secondary and higher education was relatively low. Thus, encouragement "to keep to your home" remained the norm for most women; nevertheless, the Spanish woman was on the threshold of a broader way of life.

In summary, the quality of life in the period from 1960 to 1975 reflected a marked increase in living standards. Spanish men and women at all levels of society benefited from a vastly changed economic structure. Prominent observers of Spanish society repeatedly express the magnitude of social transformation in those years in terms of generally improved living conditions. The factors to which they allude most often include greater economic opportunities—better living conditions, material prosperity, improved productivity, higher salaries, and better working conditions—modernized and expanded transportation, and exposure to new ideas through increased foreign contacts.

Conclusions: The Impact of Tourism During the Franco Period

During the early years of the Franco era, the government perpetuated the error of the republican regime by maintaining the traditional policy of economic isolation. By 1959, however, the need for an expansion of Spanish interests beyond national boundaries had become apparent to political leaders. In 1964, Spain initiated the first of a series of four-year development plans featuring tourism as a key industry in the development of the stagnating Spanish economy. In accordance with this plan, the government launched an aggressive campaign to attract foreign visitors into the country. Among the various endeavors undertaken at that time were systematic improvements in the transportation system, the highways, the hotels, and the delivery of service to tourists.

Franco's efforts were, indeed, crowned with unqualified success. Within five years after the initiation of the First Development Plan, his regime had established a thriving vacation industry that generated an annual income of some $2 billion in foreign capital brought in by the steady flow of visitors (rising to 30 million in 1975). By 1973, the financial benefits derived from this industry had combined with expanded foreign investment to transform the nation's former trade deficit of $400 million into an incredible surplus of nearly $1 billion.

The increasing wealth of the nation filtered down, in turn, to the individual income level. While the national gains had reached a zenith of $20 million in 1967 from its $7 million total in 1958, the average earnings of a Spanish worker rose steadily from $317 per year in 1960, to $850 in 1967, and to $1,250 in 1973. Not unexpectedly, increased salaries were reflected directly in expanded purchasing power, which resulted in a remarkable improvement of living conditions for the working classes.

The dramatic change brought about by the government in the economic structure of the country through its support of an externally oriented industry—tourism—brought about demographic shifts that further affected daily life in Spanish society. With the diminished role of agriculture, large numbers or rural workers migrated to the "tourist" regions, such as the Mediterranean and Balearic Islands, which offered new job opportunities. Job security and higher wages resulted eventually in the creation of a new working elite that soon adapted to, and adopted, the standards of living of the Spanish middle class. Furthermore, the increased exposure of Spaniards to foreign values and ideals resulting from the tourist trade achieved a profound and lasting effect on the people's orientation to the nation and to the rest of the world: it liberalized their political and moral thinking and generally lessened the traditional provincialism and regionalism that had restricted their horizons in the past.

On the whole, then, the economic policies of the Franco regime should be seen as not only spectacularly productive in terms of national economic expansion, but also as highly significant with respect to social change. In brief, Spain under Franco ascended from the status of an isolated, agricultural, and underdeveloped country to that of a modern, industrial, and successful state. At the same time, this economic expansion based primarily on the tourist trade also transformed Spanish society from a rural, materially deprived, and rigidly stratified community into one relatively receptive to change characterized by urbanization, a growing, prosperous middle class, and expanding opportunities for upward mobility. If one takes into consideration the other transformations that took place in Spanish society during these years—among others, the changing role and status of women and the accessibility of public education to all individuals—the impact of the Franco government on the daily life of the people must be rated as dramatic, for it provided them with the economic and social means of improving the conditions of their lives and, above all, gave them hope for a better future.

Endnotes

1. Spanish Information Service, *Fundamental Laws of the State: The Spanish Constitution* (Madrid: Sucesores de Rivadeneyra, S. A., 1968), p. 24.
2. Ibid.
3. Ibid., pp. 52–53.
4. Ibid., pp. 54–55.
5. Ibid., pp. 104–5.
6. Michael Perceval, *The Spaniards: How They Live and Work* (New York: Praeger, 1969), p. 40.
7. Benjamin Welles, *The Gentle Anarchy* (New York: Praeger, 1965), p. 324.
8. Diplomatic Information Office, "Tourism Finances Forty-two Percent of the Trade Gap," *Spain 77*, Madrid: August 1977, p. 6.
9. Welles, *The Gentle Anarchy*, p. 6.
10. Ibid., p. 325.
11. John Crow, *Spain: The Root and the Flower* (New York: Harper and Row, 1975), p. 375.
12. Ibid., p. 391.
13. Ibid., p. 392.
14. Welles, *The Gentle Anarchy*, p. 325.
15. Crow, *Spain*, p. 381.
16. Diplomatic Information Office, "The Spanish Economy in the Period 1955–75," *Spain 79*, Madrid: April 1979, p. 4.
17. Diplomatic Information Office, "Provincial Distribution of Spain's National Income," *Spain 78*, Madrid: March 1978, p. 6.
18. Crow, *Spain*, p. 408.
19. Perceval, *The Spaniards*, p. 114.
20. Ibid., p. 117.
21. Crow, *Spain*, p. 409.

22. Eugene K. Keefe, *Area Handbook for Spain* (Washington, DC: Foreign Area Studies [FAS] of the American University, U.S. Government Printing Office, 1976), p. xiii.

23. Ibid.

24. Welles, *The Gentle Anarchy*, p. 325.

25. Max Gallo, *Spain under Franco* (New York: E. P. Dutton, 1974), pp. 346–48.

26. Crow, *Spain*, p. 408.

27. Gallo, *Spain under Franco*, p. 348.

7

Regional Diversity

The description of regional particularity in the 1960–75 period depicts the impact of Franco's authoritarian rule on the traditional territories of Catalonia, the Basque Provinces, and Galicia. This regional situation, reviewed in the light of zealous political actions, focuses on three cultural factors selected to illuminate local-national relationships: the assimilation of local character, local spirit, and the status of national unity.

Political Policies

In contrast to the philosophy of the Republic, the Franco regime sought to create a strong, centralized nation with authority concentrated in the office of head of state. Consequently, throughout his regime Franco attempted to diminish the influence of regional sentiments, which had prevailed under the Republic.

In 1938, Franco initiated a series of decrees that abolished the Catalan Statute of 1932 and all laws established by the *generalitat* and forbade the use of the Catalan language in education, government, and newspapers. Subsequent decrees prohibited continuance of the virtually autonomous government of the Basques and barred the use of the Basque language in all publications. As a final blow to representation of regional interests, during the course of the Civil War Franco decreed that the public election of local officials (introduced by the Republic) would be eliminated.

The geographical makeup of the nation under Franco was established by the Organic Law of the State of January 10, 1967. Title 1, article 1, stated:

I. The Spanish State, constituted as a kingdom, is the supreme institution of the national community.
II. The State is Responsible for the exercise of sovereignty through the agencies that implement its functions.[1]

Title 1, article 2, stated:

National sovereignty is one and indivisible, and is not subject to delegation or cession.[2]

Title 8, article 47, stated:

The State promotes the development of municipal and provincial life, protects and favors the patrimony of the local corporations and ensures the economic means necessary for the fulfillment of their ends.[3]

Title 8, article 48, stated:

The system of local Administration and of its Corporations, in accordance with the provisions of the preceding articles and the guarantees demanded by the common good in this respect, shall be determined by law.[4]

In addition to centralizing administrative authority, the regime also sought steadily to concentrate economic development in Spain's metropolitan centers. Richard Herr suggested: "More deliberate was the decision to hold back the industrial areas traditionally opposed to the regime: Catalonia and the Basque provinces."[5]

The regime sought to unify the nation's financial structure by centralizing control of economic activity in Madrid. During the 1960s the government influenced major banks to draw capital investment and business into the city. In 1965, Madrid banks controlled 60 percent of the nation's capital and reserves.[6] Further, the government concentrated the construction of dams and new industries in Madrid and other cities in central Spain. The regime's First Development Plan specified seven "poles of development," four of which—Valladolid, Burgos, Zaragoza, and Seville—were located in this area.

During the course of the Civil War, Franco was proclaimed head of the Spanish state and chose to administer the country in totalitarian style. His immediate goal was to unify the nation and create a strong centralized state. Throughout his regime, his political actions in all areas served to maintain and strengthen his power. Through the elimination of autonomous regional governments, abolition of local elections, establishment of an authoritarian system, with the state as the "supreme institution," and centralization of economic development, Franco accomplished almost total government control over all aspects of Spanish life.

The Assimilation of Local Character

Although Franco's policy of strong centralized administration actively discouraged the perpetuation of distinct local identities, territorial entities such as Catalonia, the

Basque Provinces, and Galicia did succeed in maintaining their deeply ingrained regional characteristics throughout the period. The persistence of regionalism in Spain under Franco has been noted repeatedly by modern observers. There is little doubt in the minds of social scientists that the Spanish state, although centralized in political structure, was not unified as a nation. Beneath the appearance of enforced uniformity, there remained significantly conflicting views of life in local areas.

Feelings of particularism were primarily confined to the middle class. In Catalonia and the Basque area there was a relatively even distribution of property and income, fostering a greater sense of homogeneity and middle-class ethos. The middle-class cause of maintaining regional identification resumed immediately after the Civil War.

On the whole, however, certain aspects of the new social patterns tended to reinforce traditional regional tendencies that persisted during these years. To some extent, the maintenance of local fervor in the northern areas was stimulated by improved economic conditions, strong religious values, increased social activities, and a more "progressive" outlook on life in general. The fact that the northern regions preserved their lead in industrial development and *per capita* income compared to most other regions of Spain helped maintain local identification and loyalty. Thus, both horizontal and vertical divisions still persisted in Catalonia and the Basque Provinces during the Franco period.

Catalonia was by far the most populous of the distinctive regions, as indicated by reports of the National Institute of Statistics: its population increased from 3,925,779 in 1960 to 5,122,567 in 1970.[7] Catalonia is situated in the northeastern sector of the country, between the Pyrenees and the Mediterranean. The Catalan "character" reflects an aesthetic as well as an achievement orientation. The Catalan character is distinguished by industriousness, individualism, and artistic excellence. Tracing the particularistic tendencies of the regional population throughout history, the Catalan will recall with pride the vast literary output, the political successes, the educational accomplishments, the economic aggressiveness, the diffusion of local culture and institutions, and a strong, unified spirit. Undoubtedly, the survival of the Catalan language and the central administration's overt suppression of Catalan culture and education were major indices of the strength of regional feeling in that area.

In the Basque Provinces, statistics show an increase in the population from 1,773,696 in 1960 to 2,343,503 in 1970.[8] Basque nationalism began to develop in the nineteenth century, at which time the term *Euzkadi* (Basque Fatherland) was coined, along with the slogan: "God and the old laws." The isolationist stance of its people toward the state was similar to some extent to the Catalan cause, although it possessed unique features of its own. The Basques, too, are economically oriented, industrious people who resented the central power's disregard of their regional individuality. The possession of a distinct language, they claimed, legitimized their local nationalism and the right to administer their own matters.

This independence of spirit on the part of the Basques is paralleled by shrewdness of judgment in economic enterprise. The top businessmen, bankers, and industrialists in the country during the Franco era were predominantly Basques, while they had no legacy of striking literary achievements about which to boast. The Basque sector is dominated by huge factories throughout the rolling hills and narrow valleys of the region. Bilbao serves as the industrial center of Spain.

The strength of local identification in Galicia did not reach the level experienced in Catalonia and in the Basque Provinces. In contrast with the growth in population experienced by these two regions, Galicia suffered a loss in its labor force. The population in this northwestern sector of Spain, which had been 2,602,962 in 1960, was reduced to 2,583,538 by 1970.[9] Observers of the times noted that local concern with the improvement of living standards resulted in deemphasis of many traditional regional activities.

The Third Development Plan (in effect since 1973) was intended to transform Galicia from a traditional rural region to a vital industrial area. For this reason, local circumstances analogous to those of the Catalans and the Basques did not exist in the region mainly because of the economic expectations of the Gallegos. The character of Galicia and its inhabitants has been conditioned by a green countryside, farms overdivided into small holdings, and problems of rural overpopulation and poverty throughout its history. Local dialect and cultural identity emanate from their Portuguese neighbors. Galicians are aptly described as clannish and cunning people who produce satirical literature and are extremely influential in the Madrid power-structure. Spain's politicians, lawyers, and policemen during the Franco period were disproportionately Galicians, including General Franco himself.

On the whole, the local character and traditional sentiment in Catalonia, the Basque Provinces, and Galicia persisted throughout the Franco period. However, the regime's policy of developing a unitary state noticeably diminished regional activities. Nevertheless, despite Franco's attempt to establish a uniform Spanish character through political actions, Spain continued to retain its many faces as religious values, higher living standards, and strong social ties continued to reinforce local fervor in the regional areas in ways that could not be completely counteracted by government actions.

Local Spirit

As a result of political policies and economic development, several manifestations of regional spirit languished during the Franco period. The strong regional feelings that had inspired home rule movements under the Republic were systematically suppressed under Franco's rule. Observers of the era have emphasized, however, that regionalism was only dormant and, while not always expressed through overt actions, persisted throughout the Franco era. Since autonomist sentiment was quelled by the political structure, the nature of regional spirit instead centered around those fundamental cultural and economic issues that had nurtured it in the past. Regional interests were modified in response to the political and economic atmosphere of the time, rather than being eradicated by it. As part of this trend, new economic and social forces that had emerged in the era were reshaping the regional positions in ways that were not always predictable.

Local sentiments were greatly affected by the process of industrialization, which created feelings of class solidarity that, in turn, gradually took the place of geographical identification. In the late sixties strong regionalist feelings were counteracted through migratory shifts to the cities, forming heterogeneous communities where labor rights and issues were the only common concerns. Regional identification was diluted by the development of Madrid as the industrial and commercial center of the nation and the influx of peasants from the southern regions to the work force in Catalonia and the Basque areas. Andalusians and Murcianos found work in Barcelona, people from Extremadura took jobs in Madrid, and workers from the Castilian plateau joined the labor force in Bilbao.

Nevertheless, within the regional territories there remained strongholds of local spirit from which autonomist tendencies were activated in the form of strikes and demonstrations. The most vocal centers of regionalist spirit, such as Bilbao and Barcelona, also regional strongholds during the Civil War, were reluctant to reconcile their positions to Franco's policy. Traditional regionalist persistence in the era was, naturally, based on historical, political, and ethnic factors that did not always coincide logically with economic or demographic trends.

Matters rested somewhat uneasily in Catalonia. Within the boundaries of this region, incidents occurred that attested to the vitality of local spirit. Surely, the passage of time and the development of economic prosperity diluted regionalist feelings, but the Catalans were not people to relinquish completely their hopes for autonomy. During the Franco era, enough incidents did occur in the form of strikes and violent demonstrations against centralized policy to exhibit clearly that Catalan regionalistic tendencies were only dormant. However, Madrid did not hesitate to impose her authority whenever there was indication of serious local disaffection.

In the Basque Provinces, an apparent quiescence marked the Franco years, highlighted by successful centralism and economic satisfaction. However, although central authorities continued to maintain control of the regional situation in the area, the bonds of loyalty underlying Basque regionalism remained an explosive force, particularly in its support of industrial goals. The region's fierce independence and the radical aspirations of its workers distinctly indicated that Basque fervor would not permanently be put to rest.

Local consciousness in Galicia was difficult to interpret in these years. General observations were that regional interests persisted in Galicia, but that economic progress kept these activities to minimal proportions. Both the regional and central governments were committed to developing the area's meager industry and raising the local standard of living. However, two additional factors inhibited Galician spirit in this era: first, the Galicians' increasing gravitation toward the neighboring Portuguese culture; and second, their doubts that Galician cultural identity would ever receive official encouragement from the central government.

In the Franco era, then, local spirit was diluted in all three of the leading regions. Regionalist tendencies lay dormant at the time and in some respects were replaced by class identification. Accordingly, overt actions to encourage autonomous movements were kept at a minimum by the local populations during those years.

The Status of National Unity

At the outset of his regime, Franco decreed that autonomous local governments were not to be a part of the legal-administrative framework of Spain. The centralizing policies hereby established under his leadership were aimed toward the suppression of regionalist activities in an attempt to create a unitary state. Throughout the entirety of his regime, Franco went to great lengths to suppress Basque and Catalan culture.

In outlining local relations with the central government, the administration deliberately avoided all official recognition of regional particularity and local governments. Simply, the official administrative view did not acknowledge the existence of local interests, attitudes, initiative, or structure. Consequently, although regional sentiments persisted as well as resentment of central control, Spain functioned as a single political unit throughout the Franco period.

The major tactic adopted by the Caudillo in breaking down regional barriers was to centralize economic activity. Regional development was subordinated to national aims in the overall scheme of economic planning. Franco designated centers for economic growth in which he encouraged industrial development through investment incentives and subsidies. The major changes in traditional areas that emerged as a result of this selective industrialization process in Spain included (a) the transposition of Madrid from the original administrative capital into a financial and industrial center; (b) dilution of regional sentiments through population shifts to cities; and (c) the evolution of feelings of economic class consciousness and solidarity. The extent to which the regime accomplished its centralization objectives was recounted comprehensively by Herr:

> The entire process was . . . creating a more centralized and unified national economy, transforming the structure inherited from the Moderado period . . . Just as roads, telephones, and electric power lines were welding the separate geographic regions into one interconnected economic unit, and migrations were filling the cities with workers from all parts of the country, government agencies, banks, and corporations were producing a simple interlocking elite of state officials, bankers, and corporation executives, highly concentrated in Madrid. In a very real sense the regionalism which had marked Spain since medieval times was under mortal attack.[10]

In summary, then, the Franco regime did not officially recognize regional governments, cultures, or interests throughout its entire duration. Consequently, despite the persistence of deeply rooted local sentiments, autonomous states did not achieve full stature, for they were not permitted official sanction in the political framework of that period. From 1960 on, Franco relied heavily on economic policies to strengthen his central government and discourage all regional diversification.

Conclusions: National Integration During the Franco Period

Clearly, Franco's authoritarian rule was manifested through the promotion of a universal orientation enforced throughout all regions. From the beginning of his regime, Franco discouraged the perpetuation of local independence. His administration, therefore, sought to unify the political structure primarily through the elimination of autonomous regional governments and centralization of economic development. Accordingly, Franco decreed that local governments were not permitted in the political-administrative framework in Spain. In addition, he deliberately discouraged regional sentiments by ignoring local activities and characteristics. In fact, Franco initiated legislation prohibiting legal representation of regional interests during the course of the Civil War. The consolidation of administrative authority under the regime was established by the Organic Law of the State. As a result, the political and social structures of Catalonia, the Basque Provinces, and Galicia, previously distinct from the general character of Spain, were eventually forced to merge with the national community during the Franco years.

The regime also sought steadily to promote national unity through the centralized control of all economic activities. Franco's primary strategy to break down regional barriers was promotion of financial and industrial development in the central cities in Spain, thereby ensuring that Madrid would become the focus of economic development as well as the nation's metropolitan center and seat of government.

As a result of these measures, Franco did succeed in diminishing appreciably all regional activities. Little by little, the superficial components of local culture appeared to move closer to the collective character of the nation at that time, as a result of reduced overt actions for local independence. In reality, however, it would appear that traditional sentiment was only dormant during this period. As noted by numerous observers, despite the pressures to form a uniform Spanish character and the measures initiated to discourage the perpetuation of distinct regional identities, traditional territorial divisions did retain many of their deeply rooted characteristics under Franco. These were manifested in the continuance of a separate language and religious, educational, and economic interests in each region. To some extent, certain aspects of the new societal patterns stimulated by governmental policies tended to support regional tendencies, such as diversified social activities, liberalized attitudes, and improved living standards. It is significant to note, however, that feelings of particularism were primarily confined to the middle class.

In fact, Spain achieved the status of a single political unit throughout the Franco period. It may be stated that although central policies did keep regional spirit under control during these years, nevertheless, they did not succeed in uprooting sentiments altogether. Regional tendencies can be more accurately viewed as undergoing modification in response to the political and social atmosphere of the times rather than the expected eradication intended by the government.

Franco, then, may be said to have achieved his goal of national unification, albeit in a manner consistent with the proud, independent spirit of the territorial Spaniard—a Spanish citizen at large, yet a citizen first of his own regional territory.

Endnotes

1. Spanish Information Service, *Fundamental Laws of the State: The Spanish Constitution* (Madrid: Sucesores de Rivadeneyra, S. A., 1968), p. 61.
2. Ibid.
3. Ibid., p. 83.
4. Ibid., pp. 83–84.
5. Richard Herr, *Spain* (Englewood Cliffs, NJ: Prentice Hall, 1971), p. 244.
6. Ibid., p. 246.
7. Instituto Nacional de Estadística, *Censo de la población de España 1970*, vol. 1 (Madrid: 1970), p. xvi.
8. Ibid.
9. Ibid.
10. Herr, *Spain*, pp. 246–47.

8

Church Relationships

As in the past, Roman Catholicism deeply affected the lives of most Spaniards in the 1960–75 period. The influence of the Catholic church during the Franco era is reviewed in terms of its relationships with the people and with the state. The investigation following an overview of Franco's policies on religion focuses on four factors: attendance at mass, memberships in the religious orders, contacts with the clergy, and religious sentiments.

Political Policies

During the course of the Civil War (1936–39), while establishing himself as supreme commander of the state, Franco declared that the Spain of the future was to be Catholic. Consequently, the anticlerical legislation of the republican regime was speedily revoked. Thus, determined to restore the congruence of church and state in the governing of the nation, Franco restored Catholicism as the official state religion when he came to power and returned authority to the church in such matters as baptism, worship, burial, and education.

In the campaign to reestablish Catholicism as the state religion, the government enacted major additional legislation reinforcing its support of the church. Franco's views regarding the rights and privileges of the church were defined in the Fundamental Laws of the State. Title 1, chapter 1, article 6, of the Statute Law of the Spanish People (Fuero de los Españoles) of July 17, 1945, amended by the Organic Law of the State of January 10, 1967, stated:

> The profession and practice of the Catholic religion, which is the religion of the Spanish State, shall enjoy official support. The state shall assume the responsibility of protecting religious freedom, which shall be guaranteed by an efficacious juridical machinery, which, at the same time, shall safeguard morals and public order.[1]

It would appear that the issue of religious freedom in the Franco era attracted a great deal of political attention before the amendment of article 6. Formerly, this article stated: "No one will be molested for his religious beliefs or in the private exercise of his cult," but that "ceremonies or external manifestations other than those of the Catholic faith would not be permitted."[2] However, in 1967 the government passed the Bill of Religious Freedom, which decreed that the state would guarantee religious freedom in accordance with the decisions of Vatican Council II, thus setting the stage for amendment of article 6.

Article 1 of the Law of Succession in the Headship of State of July 26, 1947, amended by the Organic Law of the State of January 10, 1967, further reinforced the return of Catholic dominance and authoritarian administration by stating that "Spain, as a political unit, is a Catholic, social and representative State, which, in keeping with her tradition, declares herself constituted into a Kingdom."[3] Article 32, point 2, of the Organic Law stated: "Ecclesiastical jurisdiction shall be in accordance with the provisions of the Concordat with the Holy See."[4] According to the Concordat of August 27, 1953: "The State recognizes and respects the exclusive competence of the Tribunals of the Church for those offenses that only violate Ecclesiastical Law."[5]

In summary, from the beginning the official policy of the Franco administration was to restore Catholicism as the state religion, hence repealing the Republic's anticlerical laws and enacting legislation that reestablished the traditional bonds between church and state. Franco's campaign to reaffirm the supremacy of Catholic dogma resulted in a body of laws securing Roman Catholicism as the "one true faith" of the nation, official support of the church by the state, religious freedom limited to registration for external expression, church doctrine as framework for all national policy-making, matrimony as indissoluble, assistance, protection, and encouragement of church institutions by the state, and the Concordat of 1953 as guide for ecclesiastical jurisdiction.

Attendance at Mass

Scholars who have studied the Franco era have concluded that the vast majority of Spaniards at that time still considered themselves Catholics. While Catholicism could no longer be counted as a major influence on Spanish culture during those years, it did continue to maintain a strong "nostalgic hold" on most of the people. This view is substantiated by the negligible size of the non-Catholic population in Spain, estimated at around 40,000—1,000 to 3,000 Muslims, 5,000 to 8,000 Jews, and 30,000 to 35,000 Protestants.[6]

The general consensus of observers, however, is that Catholicism persisted only in a nominal manner and that only 25 to 33 percent of the members of the Catholic community actively engaged in religious practice. Assuredly, religious practice varied greatly in the Franco period—high in the Basque Provinces, low in Andalusia, consistent among the middle class, sporadic among the urban proletariat.

Many observers have alluded to undercurrents of "de-Christianization" and anticlericalism in describing religious affiliation under Franco. Their effect on Catholicism was noted by the Spanish scholar Enrique Miret Magdalena: "The process of cultural nationalization, technical development, along with the sociological eradication that emigration produces, are three factors that, directly or indirectly, produce a religious descent evident in the country."[7] In 1967, Cardinal Bueno Monreal reported that "there is an alarming process of de-Christianization . . . especially among the industrial workers . . . the practice of Sunday mass oscillates among them from 2% to 10% according to zones."[8]

Yet, at the same time, a number of reports indicate that attendance at mass was slightly greater proportionately in the 1960–75 period than it had been thirty years previously. This apparent discrepancy was inevitably a direct outcome of the Civil War. Simply, the harsh realities of the 1936–39 war made Spaniards more appreciative of moral and spiritual needs. It was noted that even among the Spanish proletariat of the 1960s, attendance at mass seemed slightly higher than in the 1930s:

> The Catholic was horrified to learn that on Sunday, 11 February 1962, only 28 percent of Málaga went to mass . . . but if the memories of people do not deceive them, 28 percent is a much higher proportion than was then common—between 50 and 100 percent higher.[9]

111

While there are no reliable statistics on mass attendance, it is clear that sex, environment, and social class
were chief factors in determining attendance at mass. Statistical surveys consistently show that women practiced their
religion more faithfully than did men. It was reported that
in the rural areas of Castile, 75 percent of the female population and 50 percent of the male went to mass on a regular
basis.[10] An inquiry conducted in the city of Málaga in 1962
showed that 32 percent of women and 24 percent of men
attended mass regularly.[11]

The Basques and Catalans have been consistently
noted for the intensity of their religious involvement. In
both of these regions religious sentiment and practice were
more intense than was the national norm. The degree of
religious participation among the Basques was much
higher than that of the Catalans, evidently due to traditional working-class aversion to the church and the large
assemblage of unskilled workers in the Barcelona and Tarragona areas. In the Basque stronghold of Bilbao, average
attendance at mass during the Franco period was around
50 percent, although that city's population had doubled
with the influx of non-Basque workers.[12]

The interaction of social class and religious participation during the Franco era was clearly visible. The official
record shows strong correspondence between working-
class orientation and ecclesiastical neglect. A study of religious practice in Albacete showed that church absenteeism
was the highest among the unskilled workers (87 percent)
and the lowest among university graduates (33 percent).[13]
Results of a survey taken of the predominantly working-
class surroundings of Barcelona indicated that fewer than
3 percent of the people went to mass regularly, as compared
to between 30 and 40 percent in the middle-class suburbs
of Madrid.[14] Overall, it was reported that in the industrial

outskirts of the large cities throughout Spain, only 5 to 10 percent of the work force attended mass on a consistent basis.[15]

Participation in religious activities during the Franco period was also related to such factors as education and residence. A study carried out by Magdalena during the 1966–67 academic year revealed that most university students (71 percent) believed in religious practice, but that half of these students (50.2 percent) worshipped "by custom" only. Hence, according to this inquiry, external practice of religion was still relatively high in the universities, although steady decrease of such practice was noticeable.[16]

Variations in church attendance were also reported between rural and urban populations. The inquiry into religious practice in the Albacete area in October 1968 indicated that 44 percent of the city's population attended mass regularly, compared to 23 percent in surrounding villages. Similar investigations in Barcelona indicated that the immigrants from the provincial towns and villages of Andalusia and Extremadura refrained from attending mass rather than the city-bred residents.[17]

The evidence on church attendance is somewhat contradictory. On the one hand, it seems that the practicing non-Catholic population in Spain grew in size during the Franco years as a result of the enactment of liberalized laws on religious freedom. On the other hand, as stated by some observers, religious fervor decreased during the years 1960–75 as a result of the "de-Christianization" effects and anticlericalism of the regime. Yet prominent scholars have produced figures indicating that church attendance was proportionately greater in the Franco era than during the republican years. It appeared that even among the lower classes, Catholicism was regaining ground, and some 25 to 33 percent of the Catholic population did practice their religion faithfully at that time. Under the circumstances, one may only accept with some reservation the conclusion that a higher proportion of the population at all levels of society was concerned with religion in the Franco period than at any time in the past.

Memberships in the Religious Orders

As noted earlier, the ratio of priests to laity had been on the decline in Spain for two centuries, and the process continued under Franco. In fact, the popular view of Spain as a nation "riddled" with priests is not supported by statistical analyses of the Franco period. Although the church hierarchy on the whole had maintained a conservative orientation, both the number and outlook of priests had changed.

It was reported that in 1957, in a population of almost 30 million, there were 27,372 priests—a proportion of 1 priest to every 1,264 inhabitants. However, relative to the female religious orders, for the first half of the Franco regime there had been an increase in memberships.[18] One survey indicated that in the late 1960s the number of priests in Spain numbered about 25,000—approximately 1 priest per 1,200 of the population, a ratio considered to be about average for the whole of Western Europe, but below average compared to Ireland, France, and Italy.[19] A reliable estimate of that decade was that there were 26,000 priests (mostly secular), 83,000 nuns, and 25,000 monks, with the nuns and monks primarily involved in nursing and teaching.[20]

Religious vocations in Spain suffered a sharp decline during the Franco years. In notable fashion "religious clientele" were returning to lay life. Statistical data also indicate that the number of seminarists steadily decreased throughout the period. In a survey of 65 dioceses consulted in the 1960s, 80 percent reported that the number of priests ordained had diminished. It was reported that the number of theology students leaving the seminary had grown from 2,800 in 1959 to 3,857 in 1966.[21]

Demographic changes were taking place within the clergy as well at that time. Prior to the Franco era, a high proportion of priests originated in lower-class backgrounds. However, as the rural population diminished, the number of priests from poorer environments declined while the ratio of clergy from the middle classes increased. The age distribution of the Spanish clergy was also anomalous. In the late 1960s, although members of the church hierarchy were the oldest in Europe, Spanish priests were, in fact, the youngest. A survey revealed that in 1967, 45 percent of Spain's priests were under forty.[22]

Geographical distribution of clergy also changed significantly. The apportionment of priests varied greatly according to geographical districts. The proportional relation of priests to population was highest in the northern, wealthier regions—about 1 priest to every 500 inhabitants. There were fewer priests in the poorer southern regions—about 1 to every 3,000 inhabitants.[23] Similarly, there were inconsistencies in the distribution of the clergy among parishes, as noted by Magdalena:

> There are grave problems, as the irregular distribution of the clergy in the country: there are 44% of the dioceses where priests are a surplus and 40% where there is a deficiency. In the majority of the dioceses where there is an abundance of priests there are many who have less than 100 faithful parishioners in their congregation . . . In most of the dioceses where priests are needed, there are many who have to take care of 10,000 parishioners.[24]

In summary, the process of decline in the male religious community continued during the Franco era. It has been estimated that total memberships in religious orders (priests, monks, and nuns) averaged about 133,000 in these years. The ratio of priests to laity at this time reached 1 to every 1,200 inhabitants, which was comparable to that of other "Catholic countries" in Europe. Statistical evidence indicates conclusively that vocations in religious life decreased substantially during the Franco regime, with an attrition rate in seminaries reaching its peak during these years, except in the middle class, where the number of priests increased.

Contacts with the Clergy

Traditionally, the Spanish clergy had been closely associated with the elite classes. Working-class Spaniards demonstrated apathy and hostility toward the church and usually resisted all clerical contacts. However, from 1960 to 1975, this traditional pattern began to change as relationships improved and contacts increased between the clergy and the lower classes.

In an effort to address the needs of the people, priests began to adopt a less conservative stance in their work and to interact more closely with their parishioners. This improvement in the relationship between priests and the working people may be attributed to the influence of several factors: Vatican Council II (1962), the pressures of lay-religious groups, the sincere attempts of some clergy to resolve social problems, the identification of the younger priests with the lower classes, and the less aristocratic background of new priests.

Essentially, the aim of Vatican Council II was to "clean up" the traditional clutter in church matters. It advocated the separation of church and state in Spain and, in an attempt to modernize traditional religion, favored modifications in such important matters as liturgy, ecclesiastical authority, and Catholic attitudes toward Jews and Protestants.

The efforts of two lay-religious organizations—Catholic Action and Opus Dei—in contributing to the modification of traditional trends in religious matters were equally significant. They supplemented the work of the Catholic church in Spain by enforcing the principles declared in papal encyclicals. Catholic groups strongly supported church reforms advocated by the Vatican. Catholic Action, with a membership of a half-million Spaniards, was considered the main avenue for the church's apostolic action. The organization's main functions were to promote Catholicism in general and to act as a pressure group aimed at reforming the church from within. Likewise, Opus Dei, with politically conservative roots, wanted to see Spain modernized while maintaining its traditional Catholic orientation.

Many priests were actively engaged in confronting social problems during the Franco years. Clergymen tried to adjust their goals through direct contact with working-class parishioners, by lending social support and sometimes political commitment and through discussion groups in middle-class environments on such controversial and relevant topics as sex, birth control, and divorce. In a specific account of the clergy's responsiveness to community concerns, one observer noted that "in May, 1960, 335 Basque priests signed and handed to the bishops of the four Basque provinces (Álava, Guipúzcoa, Vizcaya, and Navarra) a circular letter denouncing police brutality and the continuing suppression of human rights."[25] Throughout the country, some sectors of the church had done much to improve wages and working conditions for both industrial and farm workers.

The liberalized attitudes of the new clergy were reflected in open association with the people. Young priests were more in touch with their parishioners than were their older colleagues and identified more readily with working-class problems and provided channels through which the poor could express their religious and social attitudes. Consequently, the younger priests' outlook on church / community relationships was not always shared by the senior clergy who continued to uphold tradition. Clearly, there existed a substantial cleavage of outlook between the older priests of the pre–Civil War generation and the younger clergy, who were more open-minded and supportive of the notions of Vatican Council II. On the whole, however, the winds of progress were gaining ground, and the results were that the younger, more eclectic bishops and priests, sympathetic to the needs of the working classes and inspired by modifications initiated by the Vatican, inserted fresh life into the Spanish church.

Within the traditional structure of the Catholic church, most priests came from lower-class environments and were not attuned to the problems of middle-class, urban parishioners, who represented a large percentage of the Catholic community. In the later part of the Franco period, the number of young clergymen of middle-class backgrounds and enlightened outlook surpassed that of the previous generation. Under these circumstances, young priests no longer felt alien to the people of the cities, as had clergymen of past generations. The new relationship between priests and populace during this period resulted in the clergy's support of the urban proletariat in their social struggles.

Thus, between 1960 and 1975 traditional patterns in the Catholic church gradually gave way to liberalized factions. The efforts of the clergy—especially among its younger members—to resolve religious and social problems resulted in part in an increase of close contacts between priests and the general population. During the Franco period more priests lived in close association with their parishioners than ever before.

Religious Sentiments

Nourished by its traditional roots, Spain was officially a Catholic country under the Franco regime. In many respects, spiritual life continued much as it had under more traditional regimes. Spain had always been a nation of regional and attitudinal diversities, and the Catholic church had historically represented the only nucleus to which all of these entities conformed to some extent. True to their character, Spaniards demonstrated religious sentiments during the Franco era that encompassed a wide range of variations and contradictions; nevertheless, Catholicism remained for them, both directly and indirectly, a significant part of their identity and way of life.

In order to interpret accurately the religious question during the Franco years one must give particular attention to the ramifications of anticlericalism throughout all levels of Spanish society. Opposition to the church, originating in the very nature of the Spanish character, had grown with historical developments that pitted political against clerical factors. It seemed that anticlericalism in Spain arose in part from the longtime association of the Catholic church with the privileged class. For hundreds of years, the church was identified with the crown, the military hierarchy, and the rich, while it viewed the proletarian populace as an area of defect and discontent, a perception that naturally provoked resentment among the working class. Working-class resentment was, however, aimed at a specific religious target: their criticism was not of Catholicism per se, but rather of the Spanish ecclesiastical hierarchy and its privileges.

Religious sentiments in Spain in the 1960–75 period can only be understood in a cross-sectional analysis of the total religious context, i.e., religious feelings must be considered in relation to class, region, and sex. An inquiry made by Catholic Action in the late 1950s involving a cross-section of some 15,000 working-class members indicated that 90 percent of those polled considered themselves anticlerical: 41 percent described themselves as "antireligious," while most said that they were generally "indifferent to religion."[26] Middle-class attitudes about religion were quite the contrary: most middle-class families attached great importance to religious devotion, and parents from this class were still raising their children to be devout Catholics.

With respect to the intelligentsia at the university level, marked changes occurred in the 1960s. For almost three decades the university centers were considered strongholds of the Catholic church. Yet inquiries about religious sentiments undertaken in these reputedly Catholic citadels produced surprising results: no more than 80 percent of the students surveyed at the University of Madrid accepted the existence of a supreme deity, only 61 percent believed in the preeminence of Catholicism over Protestantism, only 58 percent acknowledged the Catholic church's infallibility regarding matters of faith, and more than half of the students didn't favor the existing congruency between church and state.[27]

The curious blend of religious fervor, fanaticism, and superstition that constituted the typical attitude of Spaniards toward the church and church matters was particularly evident in the small towns. Religious ardor accompanied by the pomp of traditional song and dance usually reached its peak at the local fiesta. In the remote areas of the country, where the most contradictory religious activity took place, veneration frequently fused into superstition. While there was often a total neglect of common religious practices like attending Sunday mass and the taking of communion, there remained an extraordinary and at times zealous passion for such sacred traditions as patron saints, images, relics, holy water, colorful processions, and miraculous streams.

One unequivocal characteristic of religious feelings in Spain during the Franco era was the fact that women believed in and adhered to their religion more strongly than men. In 1966, a group of women graduates took a survey of young females in Madrid regarding their beliefs, thoughts, and ambitions on pertinent social issues:

> They noted . . . that women of Madrid respected the institution of the family, that their sexual morals and ideals were of the highest order, that they were religious (99 percent claimed a belief of God, but only 56 percent a good knowledge of the tenets of Catholicism), and benevolent, and generous.[28]

In summary, it may be concluded that although it varied according to class, region, and sex, religion remained a significant part of the Spanish way of life. The Catholic religion, while it no longer was considered a major motivating force in Spanish culture, maintained a nostalgic grip on the majority of the people. However remiss Spaniards were in practicing their religion, spiritual sentiments continued to be an essential feature of their identity and daily life. There is no evidence to indicate that, at the time of the Franco regime, religion was less important to the Spanish people than it had been in the past.

Conclusions: Church Relationships During The Franco Period

While Catholicism continued to play an important part in the Spanish way of life during the Franco years, it could no longer be considered a major influence on Spanish culture, as may be concluded from the diversity of religious feeling exhibited by the population at that time. Although the government did uphold Catholicism as the official state religion of Spain, the country inevitably developed secular tendencies as a result of its economic expansion and the ensuing changes wrought in Spanish society.

The psychological and social implications of rapid change and economic prosperity of Franco's Spain were evident and affected the spiritual attitudes of the masses considerably. Increased exposure to foreign values and ideals, combined with a rising economic independence, created among Spaniards a yearning for greater diversity in their social life. The demographic shift to urban centers created by industrialization had placed within the reach of many people a range of social activities previously inaccessible to them in rural areas. Furthermore, economic expansion had brought higher salaries, which generated impatience for material improvement and social entertainment. For the urban population, religious feasts and practices no longer represented the only source of distraction and leisure activity. These conditions gave rise to greater liberalism in religious attitudes and to a relaxation of traditional religiously based moral standards.

The undercurrents of de-Christianization coexisting with religious fervor in the Franco era were not characterized by the emotional bitterness that pervaded the republican years. Anticlerical feelings did not entirely disappear in Spanish society, but they no longer originated in government policies. Those senior clerics who were unable to change with the times continued to uphold tradition in the face of all opposition, discouraging the religious fervor of many Spaniards.

It appears that four major developments in the Spanish way of life underlined secularization during the Franco period: (a) a growing intensity of desire for economic improvement; (b) changes in attitudes and moral standards resulting from contacts with the outside world; (c) a more active and diversified social life; and (d) a perpetuation of anticlerical factors in the Spanish social structure.

Spiritual life during the Franco years, then, can only be understood in relation to those social and economic factors that emerged as a result of political action. Although observers tended to agree that sex, environment, and social class were major determinants of the degree of religious involvement, it is also evident that the emergence of secular tendencies was indeed the outcome of overall social developments. At the same time, the indices of church and social functions, school policies, and religious practice substantiate the fact that religious matters did continue to play a major role in the life of most Spaniards in spite of secular temptations. This apparent paradox may only be attributed to those physical and spiritual uncertainties that were created by emerging changes in the socioeconomic structure of Spain.

Endnotes

1. Spanish Information Service, *Fundamental Laws of the State: The Spanish Constitution* (Madrid: Sucesores de Rivadeneyra, S. A., 1968), p. 32.
2. Benjamin Welles, *The Gentle Anarchy* (New York: Praeger, 1968), p. 171.
3. Spanish Information Service, *Fundamental Laws of the State*, p. 111.
4. Ibid., p. 76.
5. Ibid.
6. Michael Perceval, *The Spaniards: How They Live and Work* (New York: Praeger, 1979), p. 63.
7. Enrique Miret Magdalena, "Panorama religioso," in Ignacio Cumuñas Solís, ed., *España: Perspectiva 1968* (Madrid: Guadiana de Publicaciones, S.A., 1968), p. 174.
8. Ibid., p. 175.
9. George Hills, *Spain* (New York: Praeger, 1970), p. 422.
10. Welles, *The Gentle Anarchy*, p. 143.
11. Hills, *Spain*, p. 422.
12. Ibid., pp. 422–23.
13. Ibid., p. 422.
14. Stephen Clissold, *Spain* (New York: Walker and Company, 1969), p. 154.
15. Welles, *The Gentle Anarchy*, p. 143.
16. Magdalena, "Panorama religioso," p. 175.
17. Hills, *Spain*, p. 422.
18. William Ebenstein, *Church and State in Franco Spain* (Princeton: Center for International Studies, Woodrow Wilson School of Public and International Affairs, Princeton University, 1960), pp. 21–25.
19. Clissold, *Spain*, pp. 148–49.
20. Perceval, *The Spaniards*, pp. 62–63.
21. Magdalena, "Panorama religioso," p. 183.
22. Max Gallo, *Spain under Franco* (New York: E. P. Dutton, 1974), p. 326.
23. Clissold, *Spain*, p. 149.
24. Magdalena, "Panorama religioso," p. 182.
25. Welles, *The Gentle Anarchy*, p. 150.
26. Clissold, *Spain*, pp. 153–54.
27. Ibid., pp. 154–55.
28. Hills, *Spain*, p. 423.

9

Educational Structure

The educational policies of the Franco regime reflected an earnest desire to improve the system in general and reduce illiteracy. To achieve these goals, education during the Franco era underwent prompt alteration affecting philosophy, curricular structure, schooling patterns, and administrative procedure. In order to assess quantitatively as well as qualitatively the development of academic institutions during this period, four factors are examined in relation to the policy emphasis of the regime: education financing, flexibility in program offerings, enrollments, and graduations from institutions of secondary and higher education.

Political Policies

While the Republic had dedicated itself vigorously to educational reform, in accordance with its own ideological perspective, Franco proceeded to act in this area with vehemence, with the single-minded intention of curtailing republican prestige in education. His primary concern was service of the schools to the newly aligned state. Franco's educational policies were designed to replace republican policies with Catholic doctrine.

Franco's first action in respect to education after the

Civil War was to close the Institución Libre de Enseñanza, which represented a progressive approach to education, condemning it for its fostering of the republican spirit. The regime specified that religion was to be a required and essential subject at all levels of education. In addition, it actively encouraged restoration of all schools of the religious orders, which had been closed by the republican administration.

In 1945, a law of primary education decreed that education was to be free in state schools and that school attendance was to be obligatory from ages six to twelve. The law also prohibited joint classes for boys and girls, whereas the Republic had created coeducational classes at all levels.

Franco's views regarding educational objectives and regulation were described in the Fundamental Laws of the State. Chapter 1, article 5, of the Statute Law of the Spanish People (Fuero de los Españoles) of July 17, 1945, amended by the Organic Law of the State of January 10, 1967, stated:

> Every Spaniard has the right to receive education and instruction, either in the family home, or in private or public centres, according to his free choice. The State shall ensure that no talent shall be neglected for lack of economic means.[1]

Chapter 2, article 23, stated:

> Parents are obliged to feed, educate and instruct their children. The State shall suspend the exercise of the patria potestad (rights and paterfamilias) or withhold such privilege from those who do not exercise it honourably, and shall transfer the guardianship and education of minors to those qualified by law to undertake this duty.[2]

Section 5 of the Labor Law (Fuero del Trabajo) of March 9, 1938, amended by the Organic Law of the State of January 10, 1967, stated:

The State shall take a special interest in the technical education of the agricultural producer, training him to carry out all the activities required by each unit of exploitation.[3]

In 1953, the regime approved general plans for school construction, and in 1956 the government started building schools in earnest. It was reported that between 1956 and 1964 the regime constructed enough classrooms to accommodate 1 million students at the elementary level.[4]

In 1956, the Ministry of Education initiated a scholarship program to provide lower-class youths with the opportunity to continue their schooling beyond the primary level. This program offered grants, in a limited number, to working-class and peasant children for secondary and technical education.

In 1962, the regime accepted the recommendations of the OECD, an international advisory organization whose major objectives were to correct economic imbalances and to improve and amplify the quality of education throughout the nation, which stressed the need for increasing expenditure for education from 1.8 percent of gross national product in 1962 to 3.3 percent of gross national product in 1967.[5]

The First Development Plan (1964) projected 334,900 million pesetas ($5,600 million) to be used for all levels of education over a four-year period.[6] The Second Development Plan (1968) provided for 67,178 million pesetas ($1,120 million) for a four-year period to be utilized primarily for secondary and technical education.[7] And, in 1969, for the first time in Spanish history, the budget proposals of the regime placed educational expenditures above all other governmental apportionments.

In 1956, the Franco regime began a program of expansion of Spanish universities. Villar Palasí, minister of education at that time, founded new universities in Barcelona,

Cáceres, Córdoba, and Madrid and created new *facultades* (schools of the university) in Santander, San Sebastián, and Badajoz. As a result of these measures, it was reported that by 1965 some 15,500 foreign students attended Spanish institutions of higher education.[8]

In 1969, the Ministry of Education published the recommendations of a study made by the UNESCO Commission on Education in Spain, encouraging free education in private or public schools for all students at the primary and the secondary levels. However, the regime made no major official enactments to implement this recommendation.

In summary, Franco's immediate concern with respect to education at the close of the Civil War was to eliminate republican influences and return to the traditional policy of stressing Catholic doctrine in the schools. Between 1936 and 1975, to ensure that the schools serve the state, the regime returned religious teaching and religious orders to the schools, actively encouraged universal education, promoted technical education, initiated school construction programs, and increased expenditure for education.

Education Financing

From the beginning, a major aim of the Franco regime was to establish universal education. The administration made clear that the primary responsibility for financing education lay with the central government. However, the 1940s proved to be a "decade of promises" in educational financing in that no funds could be found to support this massive undertaking. In actuality, Franco's effort to improve education began in the 1950s. This campaign was directed primarily at the rural towns, since illiteracy was highest in these areas. It was not until the late 1950s, the time at which Spain started to emerge from economic stagnation, that projects began to materialize and educational improvements began to progress.

By the 1960s education had became a paramount concern of most Spaniards. Expenditure for education began to increase in large proportions, notwithstanding the fact that throughout the regime, as during the republican era, the government never provided enough schools to attain its goals of educating all citizens. In the early 1960s the regime accepted the recommendations of the OECD project, establishing a program of planned financing for education. By agreeing to OECD proposals, the regime obligated itself to a progressive program of expenditure on education at fixed peseta values.

During the 1960s the economy was directed by four-year growth programs in which education received major attention. In the First Development Plan, allotments were included for education at all levels, yet the number of schools remained insufficient: "The First Development Plan made a valiant stab at this shortage, deducing a deficit of 27,000 classrooms and aiming to build 14,000 in four years. In fact, about 10,000 seem to have been built."[9] The efforts of the second plan included an appropriation of 67,178 million pesetas ($1,120 million) for the four-year period 1968–71 for the purpose of creating 1.7 million more schooling sites, mostly on the secondary and technical levels.[10]

The allotments for education increased considerably during the Franco era, to the extent that in 1969 Franco sanctioned an unprecedented budget proposal by allocating more expenditure for education than all other departments of government, including defense. Documentation of the growth in state education expenditures as a percentage of national revenues is noted in table 6.

Table 6
Percentage of Revenues Spent on Education, 1960–74*

1960	1962	1966	1968	1970	1974
1.30	1.71	1.99	2.14	2.83	2.3

*Rafael Gomez Perez, Las *Ideologías políticas ante la libertad de enseñanza* (Madrid: Editorial Dossat, S.A., 1977), p. 133.

Budgetary figures in 1968 clearly indicated that education expenditures were keeping pace with rising costs. Nevertheless, the Spanish government allocations for education were still low when compared to those of other European nations. In the mid-1960s no more than 2.4 percent of Spain's national income was devoted to educational matters, the lowest proportion in Europe and just one-half of British educational allocations.[11]

In the 1975–76 school year a government commission estimated that the expenditure for each student attending school that year was 29,000 pesetas.[12] However, the major proportion of educational expenditures was allocated to classroom construction. Although statistics on school construction in the era are not consistent, a steady increase in the number of schooling sites is evident. One set of figures estimates that between 1956 and 1964 the government constructed 25,600 classrooms to serve 1 million pupils at the primary level and that by the end of this period there were classrooms for 3.9 million students at this level in state and private institutions. It was further noted that in 1966 there existed 1,700 secondary schools, in comparison to 111 in 1936.[13]

For the 1960s as a whole, the full complement of schooling sites was reported to be 82,500 classrooms of free state schools, 17,300 fee-paying classrooms operated by religious orders, and 10,700 classrooms of private fee-paying

Table 7
Growth in Educational Expenditure, 1960–75*

Year	Growth Index
1951	100.0
1955	172.2
1960	368.2
1965	950.2
1970	2.967.0
1973	4.603.9
1975	6.659.0

*Rafael Gomez Perez, *Las Ideologías políticas ante la libertad de enseñanza* (Madrid: Editorial Dossat, S.A., 1977), p. 131.

nonreligious institutions, but nonreligious-run.[14] However indefinite figures on Spanish education might be, by the end of the 1960s many new schooling sites (mostly primary schools) were visible throughout the rural areas.

Using 100.0 as an index for the expenditure of the Ministry of Education in 1951, the increase of educational outlay from 1960 to 1965 is depicted in table 7.

From the start, then, educational financing under Franco was under central control. It was the intention of the regime to continue the school construction program initiated by the Republic. Accordingly, the government began a steady increase in the rate of spending for education, and the number of schools at all levels increased consistently between the years 1960 and 1975. As a direct consequence of the government's program of spending for education, some type of schooling was available in just about every community throughout Spain by the end of the 1960s.

Flexibility in Program Offerings

At the inception of his regime Franco abolished the liberalized curricula that characterized the republican educational system and turned to traditional content in educational programming. Dismissing the flexible pedagogical programs of the Republic, Franco established an educational format subject to strict centralized control and religious principles.

Education during this period was directed by the Ministry of Education and Science, which controlled all aspects of elementary, secondary, and university education. That is, the government controlled and directed the program offerings as well as the organizational structure of the entire educational system in Spain. As a result, course offerings for both private institutions and *colegios* (state schools) were identical.

For children from ages six to ten, education at the elementary level was free, obligatory, and sex-segregated. To enroll at the secondary level an entrance examination was required; a seven-year program and a sequence of state examinations then led to the *bachillerato*. Secondary education required several fees. Students could pursue the *bachillerato* in state schools or in private institutions operated by the religious orders. Curricula at all levels were fixed and uniform, leaving little opportunity for students to elect subjects. In all private and state schools the Roman Catholic religion was studied.

Since only elementary schools were free, a large number of students were not able to continue their education beyond the primary level for economic reasons. The options open to them in further schooling consisted of vocational training of various types, some producing skillful mechanics and technicians.

Under Franco, Catholic dogma once again became the primary basis of school curricula. This religious orientation dominated course content throughout the educational system, although several of the private institutions placed less emphasis on religious instruction than did the state schools or the schools directed by religious orders. In effect, the state guaranteed a Catholic education by making religious instruction a requirement at all primary and secondary levels. Church authority also affected teachers, who were discharged if their teaching and conduct did not concur with Catholic doctrine and standards. Bishops had the prerogative to ban books and teaching materials that were deemed adverse to Catholic principles.

The types of instructional methods in force at that time noticeably affected the entirety of Spanish education. During the 1960s classroom techniques and procedures had been largely traditional and uninspiring. Although the government was determined to extend education, it neglected to improve its quality. At all levels schools suffered from the backwardness of instructional approaches. Classrooms were overcrowded and often lacked equipment. Textbooks, which had to be endorsed by the state were generally unimaginative, and teachers remained impersonal and absolute. Even in higher education, students were conditioned to memorize rather than challenge and question. Pupils were forced to engage in study procedures designed for rote learning of prescribed materials, consistent with the traditional orientation of Catholic instruction. This regurgitation approach to learning inhibited original thought and did not prepare students effectively for career realities. Under these circumstances, it is not surprising that the quality of instruction and the level of learning in the Franco period remained low.

However, teaching procedures and textbooks began to move away from traditional norms in the later 1960s. NDEA reports for 1969 included interviews with teachers representing all levels of Spanish education who indicated that classroom techniques and texts were being modernized and, in many instances, were already on par with methods and materials used in the United States.[15] By the 1970s some of the publishing houses in Spain had recruited professional teams to update and write new texts. For the most part the new books were well planned and attractive.

Efforts to develop the Spanish university system under Franco were minimal. Even in the early 1970s the autocratic controls at the university level perpetuated the traditional scheme of organization. Professorships were occupied by men of conservative views, and the curriculum remained narrow and inadequate, with programs divided among five faculties: humanities, law, medicine, pharmacy, and science. As was the case in most European countries with a state-controlled educational system, the universities maintained a class orientation: only 1 percent of working-class Spaniards were studying at the university level.

One of the major reasons for the lack of progress noted in higher education was undoubtedly the rigidity of the traditional hierarchical structure, which discouraged initiative. Authoritarian institutional patterns tended to restrict fresh ideas and vertical movement among teachers, since they were under the control of a professor in charge. Insufficient cooperation and sharing of knowledge also characterized the university system at that time. Educational matters were always dealt with on an individual basis. Neither the senior professors nor the students possessed the right to assemble collectively to discuss curricular or structural issues. However, during the later years of the regime the government did attempt to organize all levels of education into an integrated system. As a result of social trends and pressures, the regime took measures to articulate programs and allow students to progress upward without lateral snags. In summary, soon after its inauguration the Franco regime abandoned the progressive, flexible programs of the Republic and returned to the traditional policy of a rigid, centralized, church-based curriculum. Four major features of Spanish education during the Franco era determined the nature of schooling overall. The first was state control of matters of education, which extended to curriculum as well as finance and administration. Second, throughout the system, curriculum offerings were limited and uniform, thus restricting the students' selection of courses. Third, the Catholic church was restored to a dominant role in education. Finally, education returned to an elite endeavor, where a high percentage of the students attending secondary and higher levels came from the upper social strata. In the 1960–75 period, the Spanish government eliminated liberal pedagogy and exercised authoritarian control to restore and maintain traditional policies in education.

Enrollments

The Franco regime expended considerable effort on building schools and enforcing a legal compulsory age for school attendance (fourteen) in order to provide for universal education. However, the evidence suggests that throughout the regime there remained insufficient schools to educate all children. In 1967, the Cortes referred to the absence of school sites for 1 million children.

Nevertheless, statistical data indicate that enrollments increased at all levels during these years. In short, under Franco, a larger proportion of children attended school in Spain than ever before, although the goal of *all* children was never attained. Furthermore, figures on educational development during the 1960s indicate that many leading educational indicators doubled in this decade.

The effect of educational reforms under Franco may be viewed in terms of illiteracy rates noted in different years. Reports indicate an illiteracy rate of 17 percent in 1950.[16] In 1960, illiteracy among adults was estimated to be 13 percent, although many functional illiterates appear to be included in the 87 percent considered literate at that time.[17] By 1968, illiteracy was reduced to about 5 percent.[18] At the close of the Franco regime, it was estimated that the illiteracy rate was down to 3 percent.[19] Between 1940 and 1964 illiteracy among women had declined from 28 percent to 11 percent and among men from 17 percent to 4 percent although, as in other areas of Spanish life, regional variation was evident.[20]

Statistics published by the National Institute of Statistics on children in school during the 1960s indicate that while the number of students enrolled at the primary level had increased by 45 percent in that decade, the number of students studying for the *bachillerato* at the secondary level had more than tripled. Table 8 provides an overview between the years of 1960 and 1970.

In spite of enrollment increases in the 1960s, figures showed that as late as 1962 no more than two-thirds of the children of appropriate school age reached the eighth grade.[21] Yet the 1.4 million Spanish children reported as studying in various secondary programs in March 1978 was double the number of 1960.[22] Age distribution of school attendance from 1960 to 1966 is shown in table 9.

Table 8
Statistics on Education, 1960–70*

Year	Number of Students Matriculated at Primary Level	Number of Students Matriculated at Secondary Level for Bachillerato	Number of Students Who Completed Study for Bachillerato	Number of Teachers at Primary Level	Number of Teachers at Secondary Level (Bachillerato)	Number of Centers for Bachillerato Study
1960	3,387,350	474,057	96,446	—	21,623	1,248
1964	3,762,729	745,044	128,708	107,627	—	—
1965	3,942,193	834,290	131,434	113,515	28,611	2,058
1968	4,390,000	1,199,750	—	—	35,996	2,831
1970	4,763,623	1,514,710	—	135,873	62,269	3,139

*Instituto Nacional de Estadística, *Estadísticas básicas de España: 1900–1970* (Madrid: Confederación Española de Cajas de Ahorros, 1975), pp. 391, 400, 402, 403, 414.

Table 9
Children at School and Number of School-Age Children, 1960–66*

Type of Education	Ages	Numbers at School (per 1,000 in Age Group)		
		1960–61	1963–64	1965–66
Primary Education certificate (bachillerato)	4–13	560	564	630
Secondary-vocational	10–17	160	220	282
Intermediate technical	14–17	92	107	134
and higher education (both technical and humanities)	17–24	38	50	55

*Michael Perceval, *The Spaniards: How They Live and Work* (New York: Praeger, 1969), p. 133. Reprinted by permission of Henry Holt and Co., Inc.

Table 10
Students Registered in Higher Education, 1960–67*

Academic Year	Total Registrations in Higher Education
1960–61	77,123
1962–63	88,352
1964–65	112,647
1966–67	139,300

*Michael Perceval, *The Spaniards: How They Live and Work* (New York: Praeger, 1969), p. 147. Reprinted by permission of Henry Holt and Co., Inc.

Higher education (universities and technical schools) also experienced large enrollment increases during these years. In the period from 1960 to 1967 the rate of increase almost doubled. Figures on students registered in institutions of higher education are summarized in table 10.

It is interesting that in the mid-1960s there was a heavy concentration of students in Spanish state schools at the elementary level, while at the secondary level the majority of students attended church schools. About 76 percent of elementary students attended state schools, with most of the remainder attending church schools. This ratio was reversed in secondary education, where only some 16 percent of the pupils attended state schools.[23] These proportions are readily explained by the fact that in Spain primary education was free in state schools.

As many girls as boys matriculated at the elementary level during this period, although a much smaller number of both went on to the secondary level. In the universities it was estimated that not more than one-quarter of the total student enrollment were women. Surprisingly enough, however, in the late 1960s women represented 60 percent of the students registered in philosophy and letters and 58 percent of those in technical colleges.[24]

Thus, large increases in enrollments at all levels of education were experienced in Spain between 1960 and 1975. Most notable was the rate of increase at the secondary level, which had been extremely low in previous years. Statistics furnished by the Franco regime report school attendance in 1966 at 85 percent.[25] One observer noted that by the 1971–72 academic year 93 percent of the total school-age population were attending school. In this school year, 341,414 children from six to thirteen years of age were without primary education, the lowest number reported for the years under reiew in this text.[26]

Graduations from Institutions of Secondary and Higher Education

In the 1960–75 period total student enrollments reached the highest level in Spanish history, but enrollments beyond the primary level continued to taper off proportionately. Consequently, the percentage of students actually receiving certificates from the various secondary schools, universities, and technical colleges remained low in these years.

The pattern of students' failing to continue their education beyond the elementary level had been a constant feature of Spanish education. Simply, many school-age children were needed at home to help support their families. For a large number of primary school students, then, the future could bring only a position of unskilled labor. In the 1960s approximately one-half of the students who had completed primary schooling went on to a secondary school program.

This dropout pattern was equally evident at the secondary level. In the early 1970s *bachillerato* schools experienced approximately a 50 percent dropout rate between

Table 11
Enrollments and Graduations in Higher Education, 1960–67*

Year	Total Enrollments in Higher Education	Total Graduations in Higher Education
1960–61	77,123	5,243
1962–63	88,352	5,846
1964–65	112,647	7,434
1966–67	139,300	10,600

*Michael Perceval, *The Spaniards: How They Live and Work* (New York: Praeger, 1969), p. 147. Reprinted by permission of Henry Holt and Co., Inc.

ages fourteen and seventeen as thousands of school-age children abandoned their studies to enter the work force.[27] According to the National Institute of Statistics, in 1960 there were 474,057 students matriculated in *bachillerato* schools, of whom 96,466 received certificates; in 1964, there were 745,044 matriculated, with 128,708 receiving certificates; in 1965, there were 834,290 matriculated and 131,434 receiving certificates; in 1967, there were 1,112,757 matriculated and 169,693 receiving certificates.[28]

The panorama of students not completing their studies was clearly noticeable in the university faculties. In this light, the proportion of students receiving certificates in higher education was extremely low for the period examined. An overview of the total number of students registered in and graduated from colleges and universities for the years 1960–67 is shown in table 11.

Prominent scientists and educators alike frequently pointed to the lack of educational opportunities for individuals at the lower levels of Spanish society; as previously noted, many labeled the educational system during the Franco era "elite-oriented." Education was not compulsory

Table 12
Background of Students at the Bachillerato Level, Early 1970s*

Categories	Percentage of Students from Socioeconomic Categories	Percentage of Students who Have Reached Bachillerato Superior
I	12.0	37.1
II	56.7	52.0
III	31.2	10.9

*Rafael Gomez Perez, *Las Ideologías políticas ante la libertad de enseñanza* (Madrid: Editorial Dossat, S.A., 1977), p. 20.

at the secondary level and was primarily available from church schools, which charged fees. In effect, the system favored the affluent families. The middle-class family was able to afford the fees of the church-run secondary schools, whereas the lower-class family could only aspire to send their children to one of the better state secondary schools, which were few and scattered about the country.

One study of educational development in the Franco era analyzed the background of children receiving education at the *bachillerato* level in the early 1970s with respect to three major socioeconomic categories: upper class and upper middle class; middle middle class; and lower middle class and working class. Table 12 indicates that some 37 percent of the students from the upper-class and the upper-middle-class category reached the *bachillerato superior* stage (the final phase of the *bachillerato* study), while only some 11 percent of the students from the lower-middle-class and working-class category reached this phase of study.

Under the circumstances, Catholic education continued to be associated by many with the upper classes. The exclusive attention of the church to secondary rather than elementary education indicated the class partiality of the Spanish church: secondary schools were the realm of the middle classes, while elementary schools were the habitat of the working class. Many Spaniards criticized the church for neglecting to educate the nation at large and concentrating on serving only the privileged class.

Since secondary education was not available to the masses, minimal opportunities also prevailed in higher education for the lower strata. In the latter part of the 1960s not more than 7 percent of children from working- and lower-middle-class backgrounds had access to higher education.[29] As late as the early 1970s only about 1 percent of pupils from working-class backgrounds continued their studies beyond the secondary level.[30]

In summary, the percentage of students enrolled at all levels of education reached higher proportions in the years 1960–75. It was estimated that the number of students in secondary schools and higher education more than doubled during these years. At the same time, the percentage of students obtaining certificates at these levels remained low, mainly due to the high dropout rate characteristic of Spanish education. Moreover, the large majority of students in secondary schools and in higher education came from the middle and upper classes. Observers consistently reported a lack of educational opportunities for the lower strata. As in past regimes, the educational system under Franco was oriented toward the elite.

Conclusions: Educational Orientation During the Franco Period

The nature and productivity of the educational system during the 1960–75 period must be assessed in the context of the socioeconomic circumstances that prevailed under Franco's leadership. To a large extent, educational developments were related to the patterns of social mobility that emerged at the time, among them the population shifts from rural to urban communities in response to economic expansion. In effect, the very nature of the environment made education more readily accessible to the masses than it had ever been at any time in the past. Furthermore, the Franco administration continued the effort of building schools in an attempt to attain its goal of educating all youth, resulting in the availability of schools in nearly every community throughout the country.

In combination, these two factors—urbanization and the availability of schools—achieved a measurable impact on school attendance. Educational statistics on the era showed a dramatic increase in enrollments at all levels of education; school attendance was reported to be well above 90 percent of the school-age group, by far the highest percentage in Spanish history. Most remarkable was the increase in enrollments at the secondary and university levels, which had been extremely low in the past. The illiteracy rate dropped sharply from 13 percent in 1960 to 3 percent in 1975.

It is also significant that the educational opportunities initiated by the Franco regime touched upon all classes in Spanish society. Statistical evidence indicates a substantial increase during these years in the number of students from lower strata attending schools. As in the past, however, the large majority of students enrolled in secondary schools and higher education continued to come from the middle and upper classes. Moreover, the dropout rate in all schools remained high, particularly among children from lower strata of Spanish society. Since only elementary education was free, a large number of students were unable to pursue their studies beyond this level because of economic reasons; most were also needed at home to help support their families.

Traditional inadequacies in school curricula were also evident during the period, and the rigidity of the educational structure continued to discourage initiative. Furthermore, the traditional format of education that prevailed at that time did not prepare students effectively to meet the needs of an economically expanding nation.

In spite of these shortcomings, education under Franco offered an opportunity for social advancement to those lower-class children who were able to avail themselves of those opportunities. On the whole, however, and despite significant increases in school attendance and certificate awards during these years, educational institutions did for the most part perpetuate the elitist orientation of the past. Yet, in the face of persisting class-related inequalities in educational opportunities, the children of Spain did gain some access to those institutions that could improve their chances for upward mobility. Although increased enrollments could not be interpreted as a "breakthrough" in the traditional elitism of Spanish education, they could be construed as a positive sign that the exclusive orientation that had plagued Spanish schools throughout their history was finally being altered.

Endnotes

1. Spanish Information Service, *Fundamental Laws of the State: The Spanish Constitution* (Madrid: Sucesores de Rivadeneyra, S. A., 1968), p. 31.
2. Ibid., pp. 36–37.
3. Ibid., p. 49.
4. George Hills, *Spain* (New York: Praeger, 1970), p. 359.
5. Ibid., p. 360.

6. Ibid., p. 325.
7. Ibid., p. 391.
8. Ibid., p. 359.
9. Michael Perceval, *The Spaniards: How They Live and Work* (New York: Praeger, 1979), p. 136.
10. Hills, *Spain,* p. 391.
11. Perceval, *The Spaniards,* p. 133.
12. Rafael Gomez Perez, *Las Ideologías políticas ante la libertad de enseñanza* (Madrid: Editorial Dossat, S.A., 1977), p. 132.
13. Hills, *Spain,* pp. 359–77.
14. Perceval, *The Spaniards,* p. 135.
15. EPDA Institute for Advanced Study in Spanish, *Investigaciones en civilizaciones* (Fairfield, CT: Fairfield University, Summer 1969), p. 118.
16. Perceval, *The Spaniards,* p. 132.
17. Stanley G. Payne, *Franco's Spain* (New York: Thomas Y. Crowell, 1967), p. 101.
18. Perceval, *The Spaniards,* p. 132.
19. Eugene K. Keefe, *Area Handbook for Spain* (Washington, DC: Foreign Area Studies [FAS] of the American University, U.S. Government Printing Office, 1976), p. xiii.
20. Hills, *Spain,* p. 360.
21. Payne, *Franco's Spain,* p. 101.
22. Perceval, *The Spaniards,* p. 137.
23. William Ebenstein, *Church and State in Franco Spain* (Princeton: Center for International Studies, Woodrow Wilson School of Public and International Affairs, Princeton University, 1960), p. 46.
24. Perceval, *The Spaniards,* p. 148.
25. Hills, *Spain,* p. 377.
26. Perez, *Ideologías políticas,* p. 13.
27. Ibid., p. 18.
28. Instituto Nacional de Estadística, *Estadísticas básicas de España: 1900–1970* (Madrid: Confederación Española de Cajas de Ahorros, 1975), pp. 402–3.
29. Perceval, *The Spaniards,* p. 134.
30. Keefe, *Area Handbook for Spain,* p. xiii.

10

Summary: Spanish Life Under the Franco Regime

The data recorded in part 2, focusing on tourist development, regional issues, church relationships, and educational structure during the 1960–75 period, produced a profile of the way of life in contemporary Spain. Many of the modifications experienced by Spanish society in these years could be attributed in part to the political structure and policies of the Franco regime. The evidence indicates that developments in the areas of economy, regionalism, religion, and education reflected in their evolution the political philosophy of the administration. However, to synthesize accurately the significant aspects of contemporary life in Spain, further clarification is required, which entails a review of the relationships that evolved among those social spheres during Franco's tenure as the leader of Spain.

The political and economic circumstances of the period undoubtedly influenced domestic events at all levels of the Spanish community. Franco's ambitious course of action in economic development during the 1960s was particularly instrumental in reshaping the Spanish way of life. Industrial advances in the era generated change in matters of regionalism, religion, and education, as well as the economy. The regime vigorously promoted tourism to attract foreign capital in an effort to accelerate economic growth.

Observers of the era repeatedly noted the magnitude of tourist expansion by alluding to social stratification, material prosperity, economic opportunity, and personal and national incomes. As may logically be expected, an important social development that had accompanied economic expansion was the emergence of a larger and more affluent middle class. As technological growth enabled a large number of the working population to attain middle-class standards, material prosperity in the form of larger and cleaner homes, domestic appliances, automobiles, and the like became relatively common among the people. In short, economic expansion under Franco improved the quality of life and made living conditions more comfortable for most Spaniards.

Industrialization in the era was also responsible for large demographic shifts that, in turn, created profound social changes. The regime's deliberate policy of encouraging technological and tourist expansion and de-emphasizing agricultural activities resulted in migratory movements to the cities, where jobs in industry and services were thought to offer a better way of life. Statistics indicated that during the 1960–75 period more Spaniards than ever before were living in urban environments where social life was relatively active and diversified.

The attraction of tourists exposed Spaniards to foreign ideals, values, and customs that became another profound influence on Spanish life. Modifications that evolved as a result of these influences included aspirations to earn money and enjoy a variety of material goods and leisure activity.

Economic growth similarly affected regional affiliations during the Franco period, as local interests were modified in response to the political and economic circumstances of the time. Aspects of industrial growth diluted regional feelings and actions in two respects. First, Spaniards developed a feeling of class consciousness, as industrialization created feelings of class solidarity that often replaced local identification. Second, regional interests were counteracted by the influx of workers who did not share local traditions.

The effects of economic factors on education were dramatic. Due to the increase in revenues and to the government's concern to expand educational opportunities, expenditure for education rose considerably. It is safe to say that in the Franco period some kind of schooling was available in nearly every locality. Furthermore, migration from rural to urban environments made education more accessible to a large percentage of school-age children. Statistics indicate that the proportion of students attending schools and receiving certificates was higher than ever before, although the percentage of students from lower-class backgrounds remained low in proportion to others.

In a relatively indirect manner, religious developments in these years were manifested in social and economic class interaction, as indicated by attendance at mass and clergy-lay contacts. The percentage of practicing Catholics was higher in the cities than in rural communities and in middle-class environments than in working-class environments. To some extent, then, the demographic patterns resulting from industrialization may be construed as factors that contributed to the increased religious practice in the era. Observers noted that local character also influenced religious practice; variations on church attendance were recorded among regions, with the intensity of religious involvement among the Basques and Catalans greater than that in all of the other regions in Spain.

The number of priests coming from urban, middle-class backgrounds surpassed that of the previous generation. This trend indicated that a larger number of priests identified more readily with urban parishioners. Moreover, the enlightened attitudes of the new clergy were also reflected in direct contacts with the people and in increasing efforts to offer community service and social assistance to the masses.

Thus, a careful examination of developments revealed that most modifications experienced by Spanish society in the Franco era may be attributed to the political and economic circumstances of the time. In effect, economic factors provided the nucleus of the social structure, as the ramifications of industrial development affected most domestic trends. It would appear, then, that the consideration of political and economic relationships in the 1960–75 period is indispensable to the understanding of the contemporary way of life in Spain.

PART III
Comparative Analysis of Spanish Lifeways

This part of the book compares aspects of Spanish life in respect to the cultural factors reviewed in the first two parts. This comparison is designed to assess cultural features of Spanish lifeways for the purpose of identifying potential achievements and deficiencies resulting from the transition experienced by Spanish society between 1931 and 1975.

This third part applies the data recorded earlier, which yielded two independent profiles of the Spanish way of life, to a scheme of cultural analyses that provides a precise and comprehensive description of transformation of Spanish life from traditional to contemporary modes. Hence, the impacts of economic emphasis, regional diversity, church relationships, and educational structures during the republican (1931–36) and Franco (1960–75) eras on daily life in Spain are compared to identify significant aspects of this transition for more accurate understanding of contemporary Spanish culture. The profile emerging from this comparison represents the product of changes in the Spanish way of life essential to clarifying continuing developments in social structure.

11

Economic Context: The Impact of Tourism

The respective policies of the republican and Franco regimes in the economic sphere were shaped by their political philosophies and by the specific historical circumstances in which they rose to power. Both regimes aimed to improve the quality of Spanish life through economic reform—the republicans by emphasis on agricultural reform and Franco by emphasis on the development of tourism.

A Comparative Review of Foreign Contacts

A number of economic changes that resulted from the development of tourism during the Franco period may be clearly identified. The impact of foreign capital on the Spanish way of life can best be illuminated in the context of new economic objectives, tourism as a major industry, and the impact of foreign capital on the economy.

New economic objectives. The Republic followed a traditional policy of economic isolation in its emphasis on self-sufficiency. The government emphasized agricultural reform, in no way promoting international contacts or the attraction of foreign capital. Under the Republic the largest volume of tourism occurred in 1933, when 200,346 foreign visitors entered the country. At the same time, the "growth" rate for tourism during this period decreased from 7.8 in 1932 to 4.7 in 1934.

Breaking away from traditional economic policies, Franco turned to tourism in 1960 to develop a progressive economic base. The Franco regime began to encourage foreign visitors and investors by streamlining the transportation system, increasing the number and improving the quality of lodging places, and controlling prices in restaurants and hotels. The resulting influx of foreign currency stimulated overall economic growth during that period.

Tourism as a major industry. Tourism became Spain's major industry during the years 1960 to 1975. Reports in 1975 indicated that net revenues from tourism in Spain were the highest in the world, as the number of foreign tourists increased from 6 million in 1960 to 30 million in 1975. Money spent by tourists more than doubled from 1960 to 1965 and doubled again between 1965 and 1970. From 1970 to 1973 the spending rate increased by some 61 percent. On the whole, tourism during these years was recognized as the most influential single factor in the national economy.

Impact of foreign capital on the economy. Noteworthy was the fact that the tourist industry was responsible for more than 10 percent of Spain's national income in the first half of the 1970s. Reports further indicated that the tourist industry covered some 80 percent of the trade deficit, thereby creating a favorable balance of trade with other countries.

Needless to say, the capital generated by the tourist trade affected living patterns at all levels of society. Overall, tourism improved material conditions, created new jobs, initiated the construction of new highways and air and train systems, enhanced real estate development, caused demographic shifts, and provided longer vacations, which enabled Spaniards to enjoy leisure time activities and to increase their familiarity with their own country.

A Comparative Review of Living Standards

With respect to living standards, two major developments may be attributed primarily to Franco's policies: economic indicators rose and tourist and industrial growth replaced agriculture as the dominant features of the economy.

Rise of leading economic indicators. A comparison of both eras indicates that living standards were unquestionably higher by the close of the Franco period than in earlier years. In the republican years social scientists identified Spain as an "underdeveloped" nation with a stagnant economy. Spain's economic status was characterized by widespread poverty, insufficient wages, inadequate food supplies, and, in general, living standards that observers reported as not reaching the "moderate" level.

The years between 1960 and 1975 constituted a period of substantial expansion of the Spanish economy. Franco's aggressive economic policies elevated the standard of living considerably. Leading economic indicators for these years showed continued growth, as the gross national product increased from $9.5 billion to $13.8 billion in a five-year period during the 1960s, while *per capita* income rose from $317 in 1960 to $1,250 in 1973. Reports in 1973 indicated that Spain's former trade deficit had become a surplus of almost $1 billion.

Tourism and industry as the economic base. Under the Republic, Spain suffered from traditional disabilities primarily in her lack of resources for technological development. Consequently, economic depression and low living standards were dominant in these years. Furthermore, it became evident that republican officials lacked the specific skills needed to administer the economy effectively.

In the 1960s international recommendations enhanced administrative efficiency and encouraged economic planning. These measures facilitated the initiation of long-term programs that could channel technological development and established a new economic base for the country. The Franco policies of the 1960s increased industrial activity while deliberately decreasing agricultural activity, as tourist and industrial expansion, in turn, stimulated general economic growth and raised the standard of living.

A Comparative Review of Employment

For the working population, economic development during the Franco period resulted in major shifts in both the character of the labor force and the types of occupations available to the population.

Change in the labor force. During the republican years two-thirds of the Spanish population lived in the rural areas. The working population totaled 11 million, and agriculture accounted for most employment. Of the total working force, agriculture employed between 45 and 50 percent; industry, almost exclusively located in the north, between 22 and 26 percent; and services; about 27 percent.

As a result of the Franco regime's policy of encouraging industry and tourism and deemphasizing agricultural activity, a significant increase in industrial and service employment took place, as did a decrease in agricultural employment. In the 1960s over 2 million people left the countryside for the cities. By the end of the Franco period the work force was 13.5 million, of whom 23 percent were engaged in agriculture, 37 percent in industry, and 40 percent in services. *Occupational shifts.* The job market during the republican years reflected rural living patterns. Two million Spaniards designated as members of the upper and upper middle classes were doctors, dentists, lawyers, landowners, factory owners, industrialists, and the like; another 2 million were categorized as shopkeepers, tradesmen, and small artisans; 2.5 million worked in plants, mines, and mills, and 4.5 million were agricultural workers.

Beginning in 1960, occupations changed radically, reflecting directly the effect of tourist and industrial developments. A large number of new positions had been created in the service categories, as jobs in hotels, restaurants, museums, tourist agencies, and transportation offices accounted for about 5.4 million workers. A large number of new positions in industry were also established as a result of technological growth, as jobs in manufacturing, construction, transporting, mining, electricity, gas, water, and commerce were held by 5 million workers. Agricultural employment had decreased to 3.1 million by the end of the Franco era. A major occupational development during the same period occurred in workers holding more than one job to keep pace with new economic trends, a number estimated at 4.5 million during the 1960s, or one-third of the labor force.

A Comparative Review of the Quality of Life

During the Franco period the quality of life progressed along with economic expansion. Household conditions, social life, material prosperity, and outlook underwent significant improvement in the course of the era.

Household conditions. As noted above, under the Republic the large majority of Spaniards lived in excessive poverty. Most Spaniards lived in rural areas where wages were meager, and poor housing dominated local communities. Many village houses consisted of a single room and were characterized as "deplorable." Not more than one-third of Spanish homes had running water.

During the Franco period, household conditions were markedly improved. Demographic shifts decreased rural residence, as urban apartment living became common among the middle class. Economic development brought better wages and with them impatience for material improvement. The average family could afford more food, better clothing, and respectable furniture. Observers regarded home environments (houses and apartments) as cleaner, larger, and more comfortable at this time than at any previous period in Spanish history.

Social life. At the time of the Republic most people lived in isolated villages where they created their own entertainment, as social activities centered exclusively around the family and local events. During these years the conspicuous lack of roads, power, water, and communication with other communities and the antiquated transportation system substantially inhibited the expansion of social contacts. Time for such activities was also seriously circumscribed by long working hours and the poor conditions and lack of benefits in work environments. Agricultural workers were reported to spend ten to fourteen hours daily in the fields. Rigid class barriers existed in social activities as they did in business and labor, and the upper class demonstrated little interest in civic problems.

Social life for most Spaniards between 1960 and 1975 was relatively diversified and active. More people than ever before were living in urban environments where entertainment and leisure activities were readily available. Class barriers were less rigid, and more interest in social problems was demonstrated by the upper classes, while better conditions, higher wages, and improved benefits prevailed in most working environments. The percentage of women working and attending schools had risen, and the transportation system was modernized and expanded. More Spaniards had leisure time, took vacations, and traveled.

Material prosperity. During the republican years very few households were equipped with any kind of domestic appliances, only 10 percent of Spanish homes had telephones, and the ratio of vehicles owned was approximately 1 per 88 inhabitants. During the 1960–75 period, the Spanish people enjoyed the greatest material prosperity in the nation's history. As a result of increased exposure to other Europeans as well as that of generally rising economic trends, Spaniards yearned for a diversity of material goods. A concern for personal appearance was noticeable among middle-class youth, as young Spaniards began to spend larger portions of their incomes on clothing and jewelry. Televisions, home appliances, and cars came within the reach of the average family. By the close of the Franco period, 35 percent of the population owned refrigerators, 34 percent owned television sets, 39 percent owned washing machines, 53 percent owned their own apartments, and one of every twenty-five Spaniards owned a car.

Outlook. The attraction of foreign tourists also exposed Spaniards to Western ideals, values, and attitudes. Consequently, modifications developed relative to mode of dress, liberal political attitudes, religious freedom, moral standards, and leisure activities.

12

Regional Diversity: The Effects of Administrative Controls

Policies related to the geographic division of Spain under the new Republic may be explicitly contrasted with those of the Franco era. Legislative action of the respective governments in the area of political subdivision indicates the Republic's intention to decentralize Spain and Franco's equally firm determination to consolidate administrative authority.

A Comparative Review of Local Character

The local cultures of Catalonia, the Basque region, and Galicia, previously distinct from the general character of Spain, merged with the national community during the Franco years. Diversity of geography, culture, and living patterns had dispersed the collective character of the nation throughout Spanish history. In recognition of local sentiments, the Republic encouraged the historical tradition of regional particularism. A unique language, distinct cultural traits, a forceful local spirit, and a proud heritage comprised the basis for intense regional diversities. These identities represented a marked feature of the republican political and social structure.

While traditional regional sentiments persisted during the Franco years, regionalist activities were noticeably diminished due to Franco's efforts to create a unitary state. The dictatorial policies of the Franco administration suppressed local ideals and actions. As a result of these measures, the superficial aspects of local culture were more closely aligned with the national character under Franco than they had been during the republican era, but beneath this enforced uniformity the distinct identifications of the three regions were maintained.

Total assimilation of local cultures was prevented largely by strong religious values and a distinct social life. The people of Catalonia and the Basque region considered themselves to be more religious, more progressive, more efficient, more economically productive, and more socially active than other Spaniards. The political and social structures of Galicia, however, were more closely allied with the central government than those of Catalonia and the Basques due to a strong concern for improving local living standards.

A Comparative Review of Local Spirit

Political and economic development during the Franco years restricted local sentiments, and consequently autonomous actions, considerably.

Traditional local feelings were strong just prior to and during the republican years in the three regional centers of Catalonia, the Basque Provinces, and Galicia. The Constitution of 1931 recognized local sentiments by allowing for regional initiative and interests. The vigorous regional spirit that flourished at this time stimulated autonomist tendencies, which motivated organized home rule movements in all three regional centers.

Mobilization of regional home rule actions was not apparent during the Franco period, as overt manifestations of local spirit languished in all three regions. Franco's policy of enforced centralization coupled with intensification of industrial growth diluted local interests and actions during the Franco period. Economic factors inhibited regional interests in two respects: first, regionalist tendencies were counteracted by the influx of workers from the south who did not share local traditions; and second, class solidarity, which evolved as a result of increasing industrial development, began to supersede geographical loyalties.

In short, central policies subverted regional spirit but were not successful in eradicating it altogether. While local feelings did not produce aggressive home rule movements during this period, regionalism in Catalonia, the Basque region, and Galicia remained dormant. Persistent autonomist loyalty focused on the cultural issues of language, religion, education, and economic interest.

A Comparative Review of the National Unity

The political relationship of the three culturally distinct regions with the central government may be compared in the context of the legal-administrative format imposed by the respective regimes. The philosophy of the Republic was to follow a path of decentralization of administration, thereby promoting local movements for autonomy and encouraging local leaders to develop related statutes. The Republic's attempt to satisfy regional interests dispersed the national state in the period from 1931 to 1936.

Catalonia was the first region to produce a home rule statute and was the only region to receive official sanction of administrative autonomy by the central government. Basque consciousness was at its peak during the republican years, and while the Basque statute was never, in fact, ratified by the regime due to political delays, the official record did show that official sanction came during the Civil War. The regional interests of Galicia were also recognized and encouraged by the republican administration. A home rule statute was drawn up by the local councils, but the document never reached the central government in time for official ratification. Thus, the official record concerning the status of national unity during the republican years indicates that efforts to bring about local independence prohibited consolidation of a unitary state either in spirit or in effective political form.

At the outset of his regime Franco decreed that autonomous governments were prohibited in the administrative framework of Spain. Through deliberate actions, Franco suppressed local interests and initiative to enforce a unitary state and gave no official recognition to the concerns of Catalonia, the Basque Provinces, or Galicia as distinct from general national concerns. Franco's strategy to break down traditional regional identities was to centralize major economic activity—specifically, industrial and financial development—in the cities of central Spain. As a result of this process, Madrid became the nation's center of finance and commerce.

The evidence is conclusive that Spain functioned effectively as a single political unit throughout the 1960–75 period, although deeply rooted traditional feelings persisted and local residents resented central control.

13

Church Relationships: The Effects of Government Regulations

The religious policies of the Second Republic and the Franco regime plainly reflected the desire of both states to regulate the rights, authority, and privileges of the Catholic church. As may be expected, legislation enacted by the two administrations to accomplish this goal differed considerably and represented the particular sociopolitical circumstances and philosophies of the respective regimes. Regarding emphasis in respect to the church issue, the Republic adopted a secular position while the Franco regime returned to the traditional bonds between church and state.

A Comparative Review of Attendance at Mass

Church attendance during the Franco period indicated little change from the republican years. It was reported that during the republican years 90 percent of the population considered themselves Catholics, although the majority were Catholic in name only. Not more than one-third of the Catholic population practiced their religion regularly, as church attendance varied from 3 percent in Málaga to 80 percent in some Basque provinces. On the whole, some 20 percent of the Catholic population attended mass regularly and 60 percent were infrequent churchgoers.

Under Franco, a large majority of the population referred to themselves as Catholic as well, nominally up to 99 percent. However, as was the case under the Republic, not more than one-third engaged in regular religious practice. Sharp contrasts in church attendance prevailed, from 2 percent in suburbs of Barcelona to more than 50 percent in the Basque Provinces.

The consensus of observers was that the number of Spaniards attending mass throughout the country was slightly higher during the Franco period than in the republican years. During the 1960s a study of Málaga, a city that had always exhibited one of the lowest percentages of church attendance in the nation, reported an increase of regular churchgoers of 50 to 100 percent over the republican years. On the whole, between 25 and 33 percent of the Catholic community attended mass regularly during the Franco period, a proportion from 3 to 10 percent higher than that of the republican period.

A Comparative Review of Religious Orders

Analysis of the ecclesiastical community focused on numbers of clergy and members of religious orders to identify possible changes in religious vocations under Franco. The number of priests in relation to the total population of Spain was used as a primary indicator of modifications in the religious community.

Numbers of clergy. During the republican years there were between 32,000 and 35,000 priests in Spain, or approximately 1 priest per 725 inhabitants, a decrease in clerical members from previous generations. In addition, some 70 percent of these priests were from agricultural backgrounds. During the Franco period the decline in numbers of clergy continued and the ratio of priests to the population diminished considerably. In 1969, there were approximately 25,000 priests in Spain, or approximately 1 priest per 1,200 of the populace. The number of persons leaving the seminary increased from 2,800 in 1959 to 3,857 in 1966. Furthermore, the number of clergy from agricultural backgrounds declined, while those from middle-class environments increased.

Religious community. During the republican era the total religious community numbered from 80,000 to 85,000, including an estimated 32,000 to 35,000 priests, 36,000 to 40,000 nuns, and 8,000 to 10,000 monks. During the Franco period the religious community totaled approximately 133,000, including some 25,000 priests, 83,000 nuns, and 25,000 monks. Thus, while the number of clergy decreased, there were more nuns and monks during the Franco era than there had been during the republican years.

A Comparative Review of Clerical Contacts

The change among substantial sectors of the clergy from traditional attitudes towards the church to a new, liberalized outlook was the basis for modification in their relationships with the lay population, which emerged under Franco. During the republican period the traditional association of the clergy with the elite discouraged close contact with the masses. Indeed, the major objective of the church was to maintain traditional power and privilege, not render service to the community; accordingly, the clergy made no serious effort to associate with the masses or address social concerns. At the same time, however, in provincial communities relationships between clergy and parishioners were closer than they were in the larger cities.

Traditional patterns in church relationships diminished during the 1960–75 period as Spain experienced a marked increase in the number of clergy who were actively concerned with the problems and needs of the population. The liberalized attitudes of younger priests were significant in establishing close relationships between the church and the people. Younger ecclesiastics recognized the social problems of their parishioners, were more enlightened in their outlook on religious matters and more in touch with the masses than their older counterparts, and supported reconstruction of ecclesiastical authority according to the ideals of Vatican Council II.

The percentage of young priests from middle-class backgrounds rose considerably during the Franco period, resulting in a large segment of clergy who felt a closer identification with the urban masses. In addition, the forceful efforts of two lay groups—Catholic Action and Opus Dei—to modernize church policy furthered closer relationships with the Catholic community. At all levels of society more priests lived in close association with the local populace during the 1960–75 period than ever before.

A Comparative Review of Religious Sentiments

Analysis of religious sentiments focused on the degree of integration that prevailed within the Catholic community under the two administrations. In comparison, religious sentiments appeared to be more diversified under Franco than during the republican era, but religious fervor continued to influence Spanish living patterns significantly.

Throughout Spanish history the Catholic church had enjoyed strong social and political influence. Under the Republic, however, anticlericalism became the official policy of the government. Accustomed for centuries to strong relationships between church and state, many Spaniards regarded the Republic as antireligious as well as anticlerical. Despite the government's anticlerical policies, however, strong religious sentiments were maintained during the republican period. Frontal attacks on church property and anticlerical violence were viewed by both staunch Catholics and those who did not practice their religion consistently as persecution. In the name of protecting their religious interests, diverse segments of the Catholic community were unified, as more than three-fourths of the Catholic community mobilized against anticlerical actions. At the same time, religion continued to play an important role in Spanish daily life.

During the Franco period, despite a faltering of homogeneity within the Catholic community, strong religious sentiments were maintained, the church regained its influence in education, and Catholic doctrine and ritual continued to dominate the Spanish lifestyle. Anticlerical reaction during these years came from the people rather than from the government and was directed toward the church hierarchy rather than toward religion itself. Notable during the Franco era was the diversity of religious feelings among Catholics, which varied according to class, region, and sex. In addition, non-Catholics were guaranteed religious freedom during this period.

Catholicism, then, retained a strong nostalgic hold on the large majority of the people, however remiss they were in the formal practice of the religion. As indicated by attendance at mass, school policies, holidays, church and social functions, and political relationships, the Catholic church remained a focal point in the lives of most Spaniards throughout the Franco period.

14

Educational Structure: Productivity of the Respective Systems

In general, the policies of both the Second Republic and the Franco regime with regard to education represented an ardent desire to improve the educational system. At the same time, the Republic's intent to establish a "lay system" of education and Franco's concern to return Catholic dogma to the schools underlined their respective policies in this area.

A Comparative Review of Educational Expenditures

Both the republican and Franco regimes were committed to the provision of schooling for all children and were willing to spend freely for educational development. However, proportional allotments for specific educational items reached their highest level in Spanish history during the Franco years.

The objective of the Republic was to redevelop Spain through educational reform. The Republic was earnest in providing funds for education, particularly in the early years. In 1933, the Republic quadrupled the educational allotments of the prior regime and appropriated 6.5 percent of the national budget for education, most of which was directed toward the creation of new elementary schools. Approximately 10,000 primary schools were established during the republican years.

Educational development became a major concern of the Franco regime in 1960, as expenditures for education increased in large proportions. By the end of the decade allocations for education were higher than other appropriations for the first time in Spain's history. In 1967, 10.3 percent of the national budget went to education, and by 1975 expenditures for education increased to seven times the 1965 amount.

During the 1960s approximately 110,000 classrooms were in use, and the Franco regime claimed to have constructed 25,000 elementary schools between 1956 and 1964. While most of these schools were state schools, the government continued to subsidize Catholic education as well. The number of secondary schools for *bachillerato* study increased from 1,248 in 1960 to 3,139 in 1970. By the end of the Franco era some kind of schooling was available in most communities.

Thus, education expenditure was proportionately higher during the Franco period than during the republican years and more schools were available for students to attend than ever before. It was estimated that in the 1971–72 school year approximately, 340,000 children were without schooling, by far the lowest figure recorded up to that time.

A Comparative Review of Program Offerings

Flexibility in school programs under the two regimes was assessed through an examination of administrative control, educational philosophies, and the nature of the curriculum. A comparison of these factors indicated that major changes in educational format occurred under Franco.

Administrative control. The determination of republican officials to improve education resulted in significant deviation from traditional policies. The regime relaxed the rigid, centralized control of schools that had characterized Spanish education for many years, encouraging local jurisdiction by obligating local communities to contribute to the establishment of elementary programs and the construction of new schools. Franco returned to traditional policies in education, establishing an educational format subject to strict, centralized control of all aspects of elementary, secondary, and higher education, including finance and mediation of local interests.

Educational philosophies. The philosophy of the Republic was to encourage progressive development in education to improve its quality and to reshape the nation. The government felt that the church, which had been extremely influential in educational matters in the past, inhibited the development of new ideas and the availability of schooling to the masses. Accordingly, religion and religious instruction were taken out of the classroom and a lay system of education was established in their place.

Under Franco, Catholic dogma was restored as the base of educational policies and programs. In the traditional manner, the religious orientation again dominated education during the 1960–75 period, as the state mandated all institutions, private as well as public, to offer religion as a required subject.

Nature of the curriculum. The most innovative features of the Republic were directed toward the educational system, as the administration broadened curricula and encouraged flexibility in programming to establish a progressive outlook and increase the level of education among the masses. Major changes in educational policy included the obligation of all children to receive at least a primary education, the establishment of "pedagogical missions" where organized groups of students brought educational programs to the masses, the establishment of the Institución Libre de Enseñanza, which emphasized progressive learning techniques, as well as coeducation at all levels, summer programs, schools for Arabic studies, and widespread enthusiasm toward educational opportunities.

Franco abolished the liberalized curricula established by the Republic. Traditional inadequacies in school programs were evident throughout the Franco period, as the quality of instruction remained poor and the level of learning remained low. Under central control, curricula were limited and uniform. Course offerings were the same for both private and state schools, severely restricting student selection of subject matter. Traditional hindrances were most evident in the classrooms, which were overcrowded, ill-equipped, and managed by archaic, inappropriate, and limited administrative and instructional techniques. The Franco era was characterized by a lack of organization and articulation throughout the national educational system and lack of communication among administrators, professors, and students.

Thus, the traditional format in education as reestablished by Franco failed to prepare students effectively for either the tasks of daily life or meeting national development needs.

A Comparative Review of Enrollments

Analysis of school enrollments during the two periods examined focused on enrollment patterns and illiteracy. At all levels of education a pattern of increase in enrollments may be identified during the Franco period.

172

Enrollment patterns. During the course of the Republic the government was unable to provide enough schools to achieve its major objective of educating all children. Although enrollments were higher than those of the previous regime, only one-half of the Spanish children of school age attended school during these years. At the primary level enrollments rose from 76,074 in 1930 to 124,900 in 1935 and at the secondary level from 2,078,696 in 1930 to 2,502,322 in 1935. In 1935, 29,249 students were enrolled at the university level.

During the Franco period enrollments increased considerably at all levels of education, although the regime failed to attain its goal of universal education. Total enrollments in 1965 were 4,889,000, while by 1970 this figure had climbed to 6.5 million. In 1966, an estimated 85 percent of the children of school age attended school, while this percentage rose to 93 in 1972. The number of students matriculated at the primary level went from 3,387,350 in 1960 to 4,763,623 in 1970, in secondary schools from 474,057 in 1960 to 1,514,710 in 1970, and in higher education from 77,123 in 1961 to 139,300 in 1967.

Illiteracy. In the early years of the Republic between 30 and 50 percent of all Spaniards were estimated to be illiterate; in 1936, the reported figure was 23 percent. At the time of the Republic 25 percent of the adult population was considered illiterate. The illiteracy rate dropped sharply in the course of the Franco period, from 13 percent in 1960, to 5 percent in 1968, to 3 percent in 1975.

A Comparative Review of Graduations

During the republican years, the traditional pattern of most students' failing to pursue their education beyond the elementary level continued, as enrollments tapered off and graduations at the secondary and higher levels were proportionately low. An estimated 5 percent of those students who completed elementary programs proceeded to secondary schools, and of those who entered a secondary program, only about 23 percent went on to study at a university or technical college. There was a slight increase in certificates received from *bachillerato* schools, from 6,164 in 1931 to 7,159 in 1932. Education continued to foster an elitist outlook during the republican years, as not more than 1 percent of the students enrolled in secondary schools were from working-class backgrounds.

During the period from 1960 to 1975, both enrollments and graduations were proportionately higher than at any other time. Most notable were enrollment increases in secondary and higher education. During the 1960s the number of students in secondary schools more than tripled and the number of students in higher education more than doubled. However, the pattern of large proportions of students failing to continue their education beyond the elementary level persisted, and of those who did enter secondary and high levels of study, a large percentage dropped out. It was reported that the dropout rate in the *bachillerato* schools in the early 1970s was as high as 50 percent.

Approximately one-half of those students who completed the primary level during the 1960s enrolled in a secondary school. The number of students who received certificates from secondary schools increased from 96,446 in 1960 to 169,693 in 1967. Most graduations were from Catholic schools, as approximately 80 percent of secondary school students attended church schools. The number of students who received degrees in higher education rose from 5,243 in 1961 to 10,600 in 1967.

Despite increases in enrollment patterns and graduations, the educational system under Franco was considered "classist," as it maintained the elitist orientation of the past. Studies in the 1970s continued to show that only small percentages of students from working-class backgrounds (11 percent according to one report) finished the secondary level and only 1 percent studied beyond the secondary level. It is clear, however, that at each level of education higher percentages of students received certificates during the Franco period.

15

Summary: The Transformation of the Spanish Way of Life

In part 3 of this book, changes in the Spanish way of life were identified through a comparison of specific cultural factors during the republican and Franco years. The cultural information reported in this part, which described contemporary aspects of Spanish culture and confirmed modifications in Spanish life during the Franco period, is summarized in table 13.

Separately and interdependently, developments in the four societal spheres examined shaped the contemporary lifestyle in Spain. Tourist growth in the 1960–75 period was primarily responsible for Spain's socioeconomic development. The emergence of tourism as a major industry resulted in a dramatic change in the Spanish economic structure from a policy of independence to one of interdependence with other nations. Essentially, Franco's decision to discontinue the isolationist tradition of the past and promote spending by foreigners influenced economic development throughout the nation. In fact, the quality of life at all levels of society progressed along with economic advances.

The effects of tourist expansion were equally evident in the religious community. The analysis of religious fervor in the two periods examined indicated that although religion remained an important part of the Spanish way of life

Table 13
Comparative Analysis of Selected
Cultural Factors

Focus	Cultural Factors	Description of Factors Under the Republic (1931–36)	Description of Factors During Franco Period (1960–75) in Relation to Republican Years
Economy	IMPACT ON TOURISM		
	Foreign contacts Economic objectives	Traditional economics: self-sufficient policies	Progressive economics: promoted foreign visitation, prepared for tourist growth and industrial expansion
	Major industry	Agriculture	Tourism: grew from 6 million tourists in 1960 to 30 million in 1975

Table 13 (continued)
Comparative Analysis of Selected
Cultural Factors

Focus	Description of Factors Under the Republic (1931–36)	Description of Factors During Franco Period (1960–75) in Relation to Republican Years
Cultural Factors		
Impact of foreign capital	Minimal: traditional rural environment isolated individuals, limiting economic activity and promoting decadence	Large influx, accounting for 10 percent of national income: improved material prosperity, created new jobs, real estate development, better transportation systems, more leisure time
Living standards		
Economic indicators	Underdeveloped nation with stagnant economy, widespread poverty, and low standard of living	Substantial economic growth, improvement of living standards at all levels, continuing rise in indicators

Table 13 (continued)
Comparative Analysis of Selected
Cultural Factors

Focus	Cultural Factors	Description of Factors Under the Republic (1931–36)	Description of Factors During Franco Period (1960–75) in Relation to Republican Years
	Economic base	Agricultural development	Industry and tourism replacing agriculture
	Job Market		
	Labor force	11 million, primarily in rural environments	13.5 million, following technological growth from rural to urban areas
	Types of occupations	Agricultural sector dominated job market	Substantial increase of workers in tourist services and industry, decrease in agricultural positions
	Quality of life		
	Home conditions	Majority living in excessive poverty, poor housing	Marked improvement, housing cleaner, larger, and more comfortable

Table 13 (continued)
Comparative Analysis of Selected Cultural Factors

Focus	Cultural Factors	Description of Factors Under the Republic (1931–36)	Description of Factors During Franco Period (1960–75) in Relation to Republican Years
	Social life	Limited to family relationships and local events in rural environments	Increase in urban living; more diversified and active social life, more educational and cultural activities available
	Material goods	Few households equipped with domestic appliances	Substantial increase in possession of clothing, appliances, cars, televisions, and homes

Table 13 (continued)
Comparative Analysis of Selected Cultural Factors

Focus	Cultural Factors	Description of Factors Under the Republic (1931–36)	Description of Factors During Franco Period (1960–75) in Relation to Republican Years
	Values and ideals	Traditional ideals, concerns limited to necessities of life	Progressive ideals, assimilation of Western values relative to appearance, political and religious attitudes, moral beliefs, and leisure activities
Geography	REGIONAL DIVERSITIES		
	Assimilation of local character	Encouraged regionalism: strong identification with local history and concerns dispersing collective character of the nation	Discouraged regionalism: local activities diminished, regional interests more closely aligned with national character

Table 13 (continued)
Comparative Analysis of Selected
Cultural Factors

Focus	Cultural Factors	Description of Factors Under the Republic (1931–36)	Description of Factors During Franco Period (1960–75) in Relation to Republican Years
	Local spirit	Strong local feelings activating autonomist tendencies	Local spirit languishing, political policies diluting regional interests and feelings
	Status of national unity	Decentralized state: autonomous governments permitted	Centralized state: single political unit, autonomous governments not permitted
Religion	CHURCH RELATIONSHIPS		
	Attendance at mass	Approximately 20 percent of population attending regularly, approximately 60 percent infrequent churchgoers	Between 25 and 33 percent attending regularly, approximately 60 percent remaining infrequent churchgoers

Table 13 (continued)
Comparative Analysis of Selected
Cultural Factors

Focus	Cultural Factors	Description of Factors Under the Republic (1931–36)	Description of Factors During Franco Period (1960–75) in Relation to Republican Years
	Memberships in religious orders		
	Clergy memberships	Between 32,000 and 35,000 priests, approximately 1 per 725 inhabitants	Declined: approximately 25,000 priests, approximately 1 per 1,200 inhabitants
	Religious community	Priests, nuns, and monks numbering between 80,000 and 85,000	Increased: approximately 133,000 priests, nuns, and monks
	Clerical contacts	Traditional prestige, power, and privileges discouraging close contact with masses	New liberalized attitudes among young clergy increasing clergy-populace contact

Table 13 (continued)
Comparative Analysis of Selected
Cultural Factors

Focus	Cultural Factors	Description of Factors Under the Republic (1931–36)	Description of Factors During Franco Period (1960–75) in Relation to Republican Years
	Religious sentiments	Three-fourths of Catholic community unified against anticlericalism, religion influencing daily lives of most people	Diversity of religious feelings, lack of homogeneity within Catholic community, but continuing to influence daily lives
Education	EDUCATIONAL STRUCTURE		
	Educational expenditure	Objective to redevelop nation through education: allotments quadrupling over previous period and school construction program expanded	High expenditure continued: allotments higher than other appropriations for first time in history, and seven times greater in 1975 than in 1965

Table 13 (continued)
Comparative Analysis of Selected
Cultural Factors

Focus	Cultural Factors	Description of Factors Under the Republic (1931–36)	Description of Factors During Franco Period (1960–75) in Relation to Republican Years
	Program offerings		
	Administrative control	Deviated from traditional: removed rigid, centralized control and encouraged local jurisdiction	Return to traditional: strict, centralized control in all areas of education
	Educational philosophy	Progressive development: lay system established, religious instruction prohibited	Catholic dogma returned to dominant role, religious study obligatory in all schools

Table 13 (continued)
Comparative Analysis of Selected Cultural Factors

Focus	Cultural Factors	Description of Factors Under the Republic (1931–36)	Description of Factors During Franco Period (1960–75) in Relation to Republican Years
	Nature of curriculum	Broadened: flexible programs encouraged, programs brought to the masses	Return to traditional: limited and uniform curriculum, inappropriate teaching methods, limited choice of subjects
	Enrollments		
	Enrollment patterns	Higher than in prior regime: estimated one-half of Spanish children attended school	Substantial increase at all levels: over 90 percent of children attending school by 1970s
	Illiteracy	Estimated 30 to 50 percent of population illiterate in early years, 23 percent by 1936	Rate lowered: 13 percent of population considered illiterate in 1960, 3 percent in 1975

Table 13 (continued)
Comparative Analysis of Selected
Cultural Factors

Focus	Cultural Factors	Description of Factors Under the Republic (1931–36)	Description of Factors During Franco Period (1960–75) in Relation to Republican Years
	Graduations in secondary and higher education	Proportionately low: estimated 5 percent of students who finished primary level going on to secondary schools, increase in graduations from *bachillerato* schools from 6,164 in 1931 to 7,159 in 1932	Increase: estimated 50 percent of students who finished elementary level going on to secondary schools, number receiving certificates at secondary and higher levels doubled in period from 1960 to 1970

during the Franco years, secular practices emerging from the new economic structure inhibited religious feelings. Observers noted that a diversified urban environment, growing economic desires, and changing moral standards underlined secularization during that era.

The effects of economic development on the regional sphere were clearly noticeable. In essence, the nature of Franco's authoritarian rule was characterized by a universalistic orientation. Within the political-administrative framework of his regime, regional particularism was prohibited and national unity enforced. However, beneath the apparent unity deeply rooted regional feelings persisted, resulting in a superficial alignment of local culture with the national character. Consequently, under Franco, Spain did in fact achieve the status of a universal political unit, but traditionally dissenting factors in Catalonia, the Basque Provinces, and Galicia prevented it from gaining a coherent and unified social structure.

Notable at that time were the relationships of economic circumstances and educational factors in their combined effect on society. Understandably, the thrust of technological growth in the Franco period had a marked influence on educational development. The demographic shifts that occurred at that time increased educational opportunities for the masses. Migration from rural environments, where schools were scattered throughout immense areas, to urban environments, where education was readily accessible, resulted in a substantial increase in enrollment patterns at all educational levels. Although education in the Franco years retained its traditional elitist characteristic whereby the large majority of students attending secondary and higher levels came from the upper social sectors, increased enrollments among the lower classes lessened to some degree the class-conscious orientation of Spanish schools.

Inevitably, the implications of educational developments extended to the sphere of regional feelings. The republican regime had relaxed the central control of the schools, by encouraging local jurisdiction on elementary programs and on the construction of new schools. In accordance with his universal policies, Franco abolished the local curricula and reverted to the previous format of strictly centralized control of schools. The rigid curricula used as a basis for program offerings consequently restricted the quality of education.

Thus, the evidence revealed that new developments in the 1970–75 period resulting from tourist impact, regional control, and traditional religious and educational orientation were decisive in reshaping the patterns of Spanish life. Observers of the time repeatedly referred to factors related to tourist growth in their descriptions of living conditions, noting that the productive consequences of foreign capital and contacts were beneficial to Spaniards at all levels of society.

In summary, the general conditions of life in the Franco period must be viewed as the direct product of policies that effectively uprooted Spain from the morass of traditionalism and reflected (a) a change in the economic structure from isolationism and independence to international dependence and interaction; (b) a shift toward universalism, promoting national unity and inhibiting regional particularism; (c) a transition to secular emphasis; and (d) sponsorship of mass education rendered possible by the forces of industrialization and urbanization, which magnified educational opportunities. It may be concluded without reservation that both separately and in combination, these dimensions of development shaped the substance of contemporary life in Spain. In essence, both the way of life of each Spaniard and the collective character of the nation have become modified in response to these developments.

INDEX

adultery, 41
Agrarian Reform Law, 13, 22, 23
Agriculture: Ministry of, 18;
    during Second Republic, 11,
    13, 16, 19, 22, 23; as economic
    base, 155–157; under Franco,
    83–87, 92, 148, 157
Albacete, 112, 113
Álava, 30, 117
anarchist, 43
Andalusia, 102, 111, 113
anticlericalism: during Second
    Republic, 33, 40, 44, 48–51, 69,
    70; under Franco, 110, 111,
    113, 119, 120, 123; in
    comparison, 167, 168
Arabic, 60, 172
artisans, 20, 157
assimilation, of local character:
    during Second Republic, 4,
    28–31; under Franco, 95,
    97–101; in comparison, 161,
    162
atheist, 43, 48
attitudes: during Second Republic,
    1, 4, 16, 28, (regional) 31, 33,
    35, 70, (religious) 43, 46, 48, 69;
    under Franco, 80, 87–90,
    (regional) 104, 106, (religious)
    117–123, 150, 166, 167,
    Western, 159

autocracy, as political course, 13,
    75, 76, 82, 97, 105, 188
autonomy: during Second
    Republic, 25–28, 32–35, 55, 59,
    70; under Franco, 95, 97, 102,
    103, 105; in comparison, 162,
    163
autos, 21, 87, 88, 148, 159

Bachillerato: during Second
    Republic, 63–65; under
    Franco, 132, 136, 137, 140–142;
    in comparison, 174, 188
Badajoz, 128
banking, 89, 97, 99, 104; Bank of
    Bilbao, 83
baptism, 43, 108
Barcelona: in economy, 89, 102; in
    religious matters, 112, 113,
    165; regionalism, 29;
    university, 127
Basques: under Second Republic,
    4, 16, 19, 25, 30–34, 36, 43, 70;
    under Franco, 95–100, 102,
    103, 112; in comparison,
    160–165, 188
behavior, 3
Belearic Islands, 83, 92
bigamy, 41
Bilbao, 89, 99, 102, 112
Bill of Religious Freedom, 109

birth control, 117
bourgeoisie, 46
Britain, 17
bullfights, 21
Burgos, 97
burial, 108

Cáceres, 128
Castile, 112
Castro, Américo, 2
Catalonia, as regional center:
    during Second Republic, 4, 16,
    19, 25, 29–36, 70; under
    Franco, 95, 97–100, 102, 105,
    112; in comparison, 160–163,
    188
Catholic Action, 117, 120, 167
Catholic Church: during Second
    Republic, 38, 42, 43, 47–51, 59,
    68; relationships during
    Second Republic, 4, 5, 38–51;
    under Franco, 108, 117–119,
    132, 135, 142, 143;
    relationships under Franco,
    108–122; comparison of
    relationships, 164–168, 171
Catholicism: during Second
    Republic, 4, 38, 43, 46, 50, 51,
    69; under Franco, 108–111,
    113, 117, 119–122, 125, 128,
    133; in comparison, 164, 168
Caudillo, 104
Centralized State, political format:
    of Second Republic, 33–35;
    under Franco, 95–97; policy in
    economy under Franco,
    102–106, 163
civil service, 17
Civil War: pre-War trends,
    (economic) 14, 16, 17, 22,

(regional) 36, 162, 163,
    (religious) 43, 46; post-War
    trends, (regional) 96–98, 102,
    105, (religious) 108, 111, 118,
    (educational) 126, 128
classrooms, 133
clergy: during Second Republic,
    (contacts) 4, 38, 45–47, 69,
    (memberships) 44, 45; under
    Franco, (attitudes) 122, 150,
    (contacts) 108, 116–120,
    (memberships) 114–116; in
    comparison, 165–167
coeducation, 126, 172
colegios, 132
commerce, 19, 20, 29, 44, 85
Concordat of 1953, 109, 110
confession, 43
confirmation, 43
Constitution of 1931: economic
    policy, 11, 12, 17; educational
    policy, 55, 56, 60; regional
    policy, 26–28, 31, 33, 161;
    religious policy, 39, 40, 48, 50
Constitutive Law of Cortes, 77
construction, 19, 85, (school) 130,
    131
Córdoba, 128
Cortes: in economic matters, 12,
    77; in education, 135; in
    regional matters, 27, 34; on
    church, 38–40, 42, 47
Coruña, 31
curriculum, nature of, 171, 172, 189
cultural factors, as criteria, 3–7

decentralization, of State, 27, 28,
    33–35
dechristianization, 111, 113, 123
demographic, shifts under Franco:

economic influence, 83, 85, 86, 89, 92, 154; educational effects, 188; regional effects, 101, 102; religious effects, 115; social change, 122, 148, 158

Development Plans: First, 78, 91, 97, 127, 129; Second, 78, 127, 129; Third, 78, 100

divorce, 117

domestic appliances, 21, 87, 88, 148, 159

Domingo, Marcelino, 55, 57

dual jobs (moonlighting), 84, 157

"Economic Liberalization" 77, 78

economy: context during Second Republic, 11–24; context under Franco, 75–90; depression, 16, 17, 22, 23, 70; development, (during Second Republic) 3, 4, 5, 9, 15, 17, 18, (under Franco) 75–84, 91–93, 97, 98, 101, 123, 147–150, (in comparison) 154–156, 158, 161, 176, 188, 189; indicators, 16, 18, 82, 155; new objectives, 77, 153, 154; structure, (during Second Republic) 11, 13, 14, 70, (under Franco) 89, 92, (in comparison) 188; tourism as base, 154

education: administrative control, 3, 5, 130, 131, 134, 135, 171, 189; developments, 128–131, 136, 142, 144, 170–175, 188, 189; elitist orientation, 66, 134, 141, 143–145, 174, 175, 188; enrollments, (during Second Republic) 53, 60–63, 66, (under Franco) 125, 135–140,

143, (in comparison) 172–175, 188; financing, (during Second Republic) 5, 53, 55–58, (under Franco) 125, 128–131, 170, (in comparison) 169–171; graduations, (during Second Republic) 5, 63–65, (under Franco) 140–143, (in comparison) 173–175; Ministry of, 53, 127, 131, 132; orientation, (during Second Republic) 65, 66, (under Franco) 143–145; philosophy, in comparison, 171; productiveness, in comparison, 169–175; program offerings, (during Second Republic) 5, 58–60, (under Franco) 132–135, (in comparison) 170–172; structure, (during Second Republic) 5, 53–66, 68, 71, (under Franco) 73, 125–145, 147

electronics, 19, 78

employment, types of: during Second Republic, 3, 18–20; under Franco, 84–86; in comparison, 156, 157

European nations, 16, 20, 130, 134

Euzkadi, 99

Extremadura, 102, 113

facultades, 128, 134

fishery, 19, 85

flamenco, 21

foreign, contacts and capital: during Second Republic, 3, 11, 13–15; under Franco, 78–80, 91, 147, 148; in comparison,

153–156, 189
France, 17, 114
Franco: administrative control, 1, 6, 97, 105, 107, 188; economic policy, 75–80, 82, 91, 92, 104; regional policy, 95–97, 100, 103–105, 160–163; religious policy, 108–110, 133
Fundamental Laws of the State, 76, 109, 126

Gaceta, La, 40, 41
Galicia, as regional center: during Second Republic, 4, 25, 31–34, 36, 70; under Franco, 95, 98, 100, 103, 105; in comparison, 160–163, 188
Gallego, 31, 100
Gallo, Max, 2
Generalitat, 33, 95
Germany, 17
Gerona, 29
graduations in secondary and higher education: during Second Republic, 53, 63–65; under Franco, 125, 140–143; in comparison, 173–175. See also Education
gross national product: during Second Republic, 16, 22; under Franco, 82–84, 127, 155
Guipúzcoa, 30, 117

Head of State, 95, 97
hectares, 18
Herr, Richard, 2, 97, 104
hierarchy, of church, 46, 119
higher education: during Second Republic, 63–65; under Franco, 127, 132–135, 138, 139,

141, 143, 144; in comparison, 173–175, 188. *See also* Graduations
highways, 79, 91
Hills, George, 2
holy water, 121
home rule, 33, 34, 70, 99
household conditions: during Second Republic, 20, 21; under Franco, 88, 148; in comparison, 157–159
hotels, 79

Iberian Peninsula, 31
illiteracy rate: during Second Republic, 22, 61, 63, 66; under Franco, 125, 128, 136, 144; in comparison, 172, 173
income: during Second Republic, 16, 21, 31; under Franco, 82, 83, 89, 91, 92, 98, 130; in comparison, 159
industrialization: during Second Republic, 18, 23, 71, (background of priests) 44, (regional effects) 16, 30, (work force) 19; under Franco, (domestic development) 147–150, (economic development) 76, 77, 84, 86, 88–93, (regional effects) 97–99, 101–107, (religious effects) 122, 149; in comparison, 155–157, 162, 189
Institución Libre de Enseñanza, 55, 60, 126, 172
instructional methods, 133
investment, 97
Ireland, 114
Iribarne, Mañuel Fraga (Minister

of Tourism), 79
isolation, in national economy, 11, 14, 15, 22, 23, 75, 176, 189
Italy, 114

Jesuits, Society of, 40–42, 55, 57
Jews, 110, 117
job market: during Second Republic, 11, 23; under Franco, 75, 85, 148; in comparison, 156, 157
Junta para Ampliación de Estudios, La, 60
Justice, Ministry of, 39, 41

labor: during Second Republic, 17, 18, (discontent) 16; under Franco, 82, 84, 86, 90, (labor force) 100, (women) 90, (labor change) 156, 157; Labor Law (Fuero del Trabajo), 76, 126; Ministry of Labor, 86
language, distinct, 29–35, 106
lay system of education, 56, 58, 69, 171. See also Education
Law of Primary Education (1945), 126
Law on Principles of the National Movement, 76
Law of Religious Confessions and Congregations, 42, 55
Law of Succession in the Headship of State of 26 July, 1947, 109
leisure time, 22, 122, 148, 155, 159
Lérida, 29
life conditions during Second Republic, 20–24
lifeways, 1–7: during Second Republic, 9, 49, 53, 68–71; under Franco, 73, 84, 86, 89,

92, 147–150; comparative analysis, 151–159, 168, 176
living standards: during Second Republic, 3, 11, 15–18; under Franco, 75, 79–83, 86–93, 100, 106; in comparison, 155–159, 161, 189
local spirit: during Second Republic, 4, 25, 28, 31–33, 35, 36; under Franco, 101–107; in comparison, 161, 162
lodging: during Second Republic, 15, 23; under Franco, 79, 80, 91; in comparison, 154
Lugo, 31

Madariaga, Salvador de, 28, 29
Madrid, 89, 97, 100–102, 104, 106, 112, 121, 128, 163
Magdalena, Enrique Miret, 111, 113, 115
Málaga, 43, 111, 112, 164, 165
manufacturing, 85
marriages, 43
Marxists, 43
Masons, 43
mass, attendance: during Second Republic, 4, 38, 43, 44; under Franco, 108, 110–114, 149; in comparison, 164, 165, 168
material prosperity, 22, 87, 92, 122, 148, 158, 159
matrimony, 110
Mediterranean, Southern, 83, 92
metallurgy, 17, 19
migration, 84, 86, 88
military, 20, 89
mining, 85
mobility, 87, 88, 92
monarchy, 1923–1931, 57, 58

monks, 45, 46, 114, 116
monopolism, 19
Monreal, Bueno (Cardinal), 111
Muslims, 110
Murcianos, 102

nationalization: during Second
    Republic, 11–13, 22, 39, 40;
    under Franco, 75, 79
National Institute of Statistics: in
    education, (during Second
    Republic) 61–64, (under
    Franco) 136, 141; in
    employment, (during Second
    Republic) 19, (under Franco)
    85; population of Catalonia,
    98; tourist development, 80,
    81
national integration, under
    Franco, 105–107
national unity, state of: during
    Second Republic, 4, 25, 33–36;
    under Franco, 95, 103–107; in
    comparison, 162, 163
Navarra, 30, 117
NDEA reports, 134
New York Times, 87
nobility, 44
nuns, 45, 114, 116

occupations, types of: during
    Second Republic, 18–20,
    (opportunities) 23; under
    Franco, 84–87,
    (opportunities) 89–93; in
    comparison, 156, 157
opus dei, 117, 167
Orense, 31
Organic Law of the State, 76, 77,
    96, 105, 109, 126

Organization for Economic
    Cooperation and
    Development (OECD), 77,
    127, 119

Palasí, Villar (Minister of
    Education) 127
papal encyclicals, 117
parishioners: during Second
    Republic, 45–47; under
    Franco, 116–119
patronal saints, 121
Payne, Stanley, 1, 2, 32
"pedagogical missions," 60, 132
Per capita income, 82, 98, 155
"poles of development," 97
political corruption, 16
political policies: during Second
    Republic, (in Economy) 11–13,
    (in Education) 53–56, (in
    Geography) 25–28, (in
    Religion) 38–43; under
    Franco, (in Economy) 75–78,
    (in Education) 125–128, (in
    Geography) 95–97, (in
    Religion) 108–110
political structure, 98, 101
Pontevedra, 31
Portugal, 20, 31
Portuguese, 31, 100, 103
poverty, 15, 17, 20, 21, 24, 158
priests: during Second Republic,
    44–47; under Franco, 114–118,
    150; in comparison, 165, 166
processions, 121
productivity, 80, 82, 90, 92
program offerings, in education:
    during Second Republic, 53,
    58–60; under Franco, 125,
    132–135; in comparison,

170–172, 189. *See also*
Education
Protestants, 79, 110, 117, 120
provisional council, in education,
58
provisional government, 53
Public Instruction, Council of, 53
purchasing power, 16, 83, 91, 92
psychological factors, 49, 88, 122
Pyrenees, 98

quality of life: during Second
Republic, 3, 4, 11, 20–22;
under Franco, 75, 86–90; in
comparison, 157–159, 189

regionalism: during Second
Republic, 4, 5, 9, 70,
(diversities) 25–36; under
Franco, 73, 92, 106, 147–149,
(diversities) 95–107; effects of
administrative controls,
160–163, 188, 189
relationships, State–Church:
during Second Republic,
49–51; under Franco, 122, 123
relics, 121
religion: during Second Republic,
(memberships in relgious
orders) 4, 38, 44, 45,
(sentiments) 4, 32, 33, 38,
47–49; during Franco,
(memberships in religious
orders) 108, 114–116,
(sentiments) 108, 112, 119–122;
in comparison, (memberships
in religious orders) 165, 166,
(sentiments) 167, 168
Ríos, Fernando de (Minister of
Education), 55, 64

Ríos, Francisco Giner de Los, 60
roads, 15, 21, 23
rural: development, 22, 188;
economy, 11–15; work force,
18, 19, 23, 84–87, 92, 156, 157

San Sebastián, 128
Santander, 60, 128
secularization: under Second
Republic, 38, 41, 42, 47, 55, 56,
61, 63 69; under Franco, 122,
123; in comparison, 188, 189
self-sufficiency, 14, 75, 79
services: under Second Republic,
19; under Franco, 84–86, 91; in
comparison, 156
Seville, 97
Smith, Rhea Marsh, 1, 2
social class: during Second
Republic, 15, 19–21, 39, 64, 66;
under Franco, 84, 88, 89, 104,
112, 118, 148–150; in
comparison, 158, 159, 175
social structure, 1, 2, 20, 34–36, 123,
150, 151, 160, 161, 188
social life, 75, 122, 123, 148, 158,
159, 161
social spheres, 3–5, 153, 176, 188,
189
Spain 77, 80
spirit, local: during Second
Republic, 31–33; under
Franco, 101–103; in
comparison, 161, 162
stagnation, 129, 155
status quo, 36
Statute Law of Spanish People
(Fuero de los Españoles),
109, 126
superstition, 121

Tarragona, 29, 112
tenant farmers, 18
telephones, 20, 87, 88, 104, 159
television, 87, 88, 159
textiles, 17, 19
tourism: during Second Republic,
    4, 14, 15, 20, 23; under Franco,
    75, 78–82, 88, 91–93, 147, 148,
    (impact of) 91–93; from a
    comparative view, 154,
    (impact of) 153–159, 176;
    Minister of, 80. See also
    industrialization
Trade Unions, 77
traditional, tendencies: during
    Second Republic, 1, 3, 5, 6, 9,
    14, 15, 20–22, 35, 53, 56, 58–60,
    65, 66, 69; under Franco, 75,
    77, 79, 80, 85, 90, 97, 98, 100,
    102, 106, 110, 116–119, 123,
    128, 132–135, 145; from a
    comparative view, 154, 155,
    161, 164, 166, 167, 171–173,
    188, 189
transformation, 1, 80, 87, 89, 90, 92,
    151; lifeway factors, 176, 188,
    189. See also lifeways
transportation: during Second
    Republic, 16, 19, 21–23; under
    Franco, 78, 79, 85, 90, 91; in
    comparison, 154, 157–159
Tribunals of the Church, 110

underdeveloped nation, 15–18, 20,
    92, 155
unemployment: during Second
    Republic, 19, 22, 23; under
    Franco, 86

UNESCO, Commission on
    Education, 128
university education, 64, 65
urbanization, 84, 86, 92, 104, 144,
    158, 189

Valladolid, 97
values: during Second Republic, 1,
    3, 16; under Franco, 76, 84,
    87–89, 92, 98, 100, 122, 148; in
    comparison, 159
Vascuence, 30, 33
Vatican Council II, 109, 116–118,
    167
vehicles, 21
Vizcaya, 30, 117
vocation, religious, 45, 114

wages: during Second Republic,
    16, 17, 19; under Franco, 82,
    87, 92, 118, 122; in
    comparison, 155, 158
War, Ministry of, 19
water, 20, 21
Welles, Benjamin, 2
Western Europeans, 20, 88
Western nations, 16, 75, 79, 82
women: during Second Republic,
    21; under Franco, 112,
    (changing roles) 90, 93, 121,
    (education) 136, 139; in
    comparison, 159
work force: during Second
    Republic, 18–20, (conditions)
    21; under Franco, 84–86, 90,
    92, 156, (conditions) 87, 90

Zaragoza, 97